# FOR THE LOVE OF ANIMALS

The Story of the
National Humane Education Society

*by*
*Anna C. Briggs*

*as told to*

*Constance Clark*
*and Sharon Barnes*

POTOMAC PUBLISHING COMPANY

1990

# DEDICATION

This book is lovingly dedicated to the memory of my husband, James P. Briggs, who joyfully devoted his life to helping "all creatures great and small." May the work of our National Humane Education Society continue his tradition of compassion for many years to come.

# TABLE OF CONTENTS

# CHAPTER 1

# The Importance of A Single Starfish

In a deserted alleyway, a young dog hunts for food, pawing through garbage cans for any scrap that might keep hunger—and starvation—at bay. Dropped by careless owners by the side of a highway when he became "too much trouble," the dog is fighting to survive.

His paws bleed, scratched by shards of glass and sharp metal. He finds little to eat, only some old scraps that even a dog would not choose to eat, were there any choice.

As the night darkens, he hunts for shelter, a place where the wind might not find him. Under a car, perhaps. Or behind a row of garbage cans. There is no welcoming door to open for him, as there used to be before the day his owners loaded him in the car and left him on the side of the road.

There is nothing but fear and blackness and cold.

Chances are he will lose his battle to survive before winter is out. This beautiful creature, not much more than a puppy, will die alone, frightened, and betrayed by the humans who were responsible for him.

\* \* \* \*

In a research lab, bright, highly educated young men and women are preparing to perform surgery. They will soon sedate the frisky young kitten now held in the trembling hands of a laboratory technician. Though the technician has been working here for several months, she can't get used to seeing beautiful, healthy young animals used for experiments—especially when she knows that many of these experiments are unnecessary, redundant, or not particularly accurate.

But she needs the job. And her bosses don't seem to have any qualms about what they're doing. She hands over the kitten. She knows what they will do to it.

Quietly crying, the laboratory technician leaves the room.

Trusting and playful, the kitten taps the surgeon's finger with her little paw. Then the needle enters her body, and the process begins . . . a process that will destroy her healthy young body . . . a process that will result in a life of intense pain, all in the name of science.

\* \* \* \*

I am sorry to have to tell you these stories.

Unfortunately, they are true. And they happen over and over again, all across America, every day of every year.

To give you just one example of the scope of this tragedy, authorities estimate that 10 million puppies and kittens are put to death each year, simply because people will not spend the time or money to spay or neuter their animals.

*Ten million innocent, lovely animals—who did not ask to be born!* And who ask only for a little love, a little caring. Yet, because their numbers are so very great, we cannot give it to them.

Then there are the animals who suffer in research labs . . . in the so-called "factory farms". . . in cruel steel traps in the depths of our great forests . . . in tiny wire-mesh pens on "fur ranches," where wild animals like foxes must submit to the misery of a whole life of entrapment, just so their luxurious coats can eventually be ripped from their lifeless bodies.

It is tragic, isn't it? And the problems seem so large they're almost overwhelming.

But I refuse to allow myself to be overwhelmed. That is why I have worked to protect and save animals since I was old enough to make any difference at all. That is why I founded the National Humane Education Society. And that is why, at age 80, I have no intention of slowing down.

*Every one of us, in our own unique way, can make a difference in the lives of animals.* We cannot let despair get in the way!

Please let me share with you a story that sums up my philosophy.

\* \* \* \*

One day an old man was walking along the

beach. It was low tide, and the sand was littered with thousands of stranded starfish that the water had carried in, then left behind. The man found himself walking carefully so as not to step on any of the beautiful creatures. Since the animals still seemed to be alive, he considered picking some of them up and putting them back in the water, where they could resume their lives.

The man knew the starfish would die if left on the beach's dry sand. He reasoned that he could not possibly help them all, so he chose to do nothing.

"That's just Nature's way," he thought to himself a little sadly, then walked on.

Soon he came upon a little boy who was frantically throwing one starfish after another back into the sea.

The old man stopped. "Young man," he said, "what are you doing?"

"I'm saving the starfish," the boy said.

"Why waste your time?" the old man argued. "There are so many, you can't save them all. So what difference does it make?"

The boy stopped for just a few seconds, then bent to pick up another starfish.

"It matters to this one," he said, and hurled the starfish into the welcoming sea.

\* \* \* \*

You and I are only human. We can only do so much. And it's absolutely true that neither you nor I can save all the abandoned animals, all the animals being tortured unnecessarily in research labs, all the animals subjected to the cruelty of trappers, hunters, and factory farmers.

But we *can* help a few animals, you and I.

Maybe you can do something as small as giving a modest donation to a humane group like the National Humane Education Society, so we can continue to feed and care for the animals we house at our Peace Plantation facility.

Or maybe you can take in a stray animal . . . write a letter to your Congressman . . . or volunteer your time at a local shelter.

Right now, I'd like to ask you to do something important for the animals by reading this book.

When you do, you will get to know the dangers facing animals today. You will understand why our work at the National Humane Education Society is so important, and why I've devoted my life to it. And you will be able to decide how best you might do something for the innocent animals who ask only that we allow them to live their lives unhindered by our human cruelty.

You can play a part in making the world a better place for animals. I invite you to join me on this important journey by reading this book and taking whatever steps you can take on behalf of cats and dogs, foxes and rabbits, and yes, even the great wild beasts now disappearing from the face of our planet—the lions, elephants, tigers, and so many other magnificent creatures.

Does it matter? It certainly does. Even if it's only one lowly starfish.

# CHAPTER 2

# Cutting Life: Cruelty in the Name of Science

*"There will come a time when the world will look back on vivisection in the name of science as they do now to burning at the stake in the name of religion."*

> —Dr. Henry J. Bigelow
> Professor of Surgery
> Harvard University

One day, not too many years ago, a man came to our Peace Plantation refuge for animals, carrying a cat he obviously cherished.

This was not an unusual occurrence then, nor is it now. Animal lovers come to Peace Plantation every day, bearing precious creatures who need our help.

But this time, the story was a little different. The

man carrying the cat worked in a research laboratory where animals were used in deadly experiments. He was retiring and he wanted to make sure this particular cat, whom he had named "Sputnik," would have a good retirement, too.

Cradling the cat, the man told me that Sputnik had put in years of extraordinary service at the lab as a blood donor to the other cats. When experiments made the cats sick, Sputnik's blood would be drawn and given to them to keep them going.

Sometimes Sputnik's blood was given in vain. In fact, I'm sure that most of those poor animals got well temporarily, only to die from the experiments or to be euthanized when they were no longer needed.

Despite his years in the lab, Sputnik was one of the lucky ones—a very rare survivor indeed when you consider this sickening fact: Three animals are killed every second in laboratories in the United States, according to experts' estimates.

That means 15 innocent creatures died in the time it took you to read that sentence!

And that appalling figure does not reflect the intense suffering and the prolonged agony most of these animals must undergo . . . the unnatural, loveless lives they lead until, finally, they are put out of their misery.

Any sensitive person would surely want to stop this tide of torture. But believe me, once you've seen an animal who is a "refugee" from a research lab, you feel you *must* do something about this Government sanctioned, socially acceptable slaughter, a national disgrace that is often paid for *with your tax dollars!*

They call it "vivisection." Appropriately, it's a mean-sounding word that immediately conjures up in my mind all kinds of images of cruel treatment. The word vivisection comes from two Latin roots: "vivus," meaning life, and "sectus," meaning to cut. Vivisection is the cutting up of life, of living, conscious, feeling creatures. Today, vivisection cuts at the heart of all life, its enormous cruelty just one more symbol of the sickness of a society that does not value animals.

Every year tens of millions of living animals are legally tortured in the name of science. Is knowledge at any price really worth it? Is it necessary? Just what does it accomplish?

## How Vivisection Began

I first learned about vivisection many years ago, when my husband, an early crusader against experimentation on living beings, brought a leaflet to my attention. It showed what had happened when children in an orphanage had been subjected to experimental use of an early tuberculosis vaccine. The children suffered terrible afflictions. For many, their vision would never be normal again, and some were blind.

That was *human* torture. We don't hear a lot about that any more, and fortunately society is not likely to condone it. But what I can't understand is why our supposedly advanced society does condone animal torture on a massive scale!

Let's look at how vivisection began. As with many of our western world's practices and traditions, vivisection started with the ancient Greeks and

Romans, who used animals as substitutes for humans to learn more about the structure and function of the human body and to gain more knowledge of medical problems.

The Greek philosopher, Aristotle, observed general similarities between apes and humans. In Rome, Galen conducted vivisection experiments and dissected dead monkeys, perhaps even some apes, too. He took the information he had gathered from these experiments on animals and applied it to the treatment of humans—often with disastrous results. Many of his theories for treating diseases and injuries in humans were wrong and frequently very harmful.

Because of early vivisection, knowledge of the anatomy of human beings and many medical practices used on humans were incorrect for almost 1400 years. Imagine the pain and suffering caused by the faulty assumptions based on vivisection! The observations made from using animals were inappropriately applied to humans and actually prevented medical science from moving forward in many areas.

It was Leonardo da Vinci, the founder of the modern science of anatomy, who discovered that Galen's anatomical descriptions were incorrect. However, it took several hundred more years of documentation and effort to correct the damage that had been done. Even from the very beginning, using animals as models in place of humans did not work!

The great French mathematician and philosopher, Rene Descartes, added to the rationalization of using animal models for experimentation by promoting the theory that non-human animals don't feel pain. Their screams and groans were dismissed as no more than squeaks from a machine.

Can you imagine this unbelievable insensitivity? Have you ever heard a dog whimper in pain when his paw is accidentally stepped on? A cat's meow sounds almost like a scream as her tail is caught in a door? It's hard to believe that these learned European surgeons and scientists could use this as a justification for horrible experiments carried out on animals in biomedical research during the latter part of the 19th century.

Tragically, though, this horrifying practice has not diminished in modern times, but has grown into a multi-million dollar research industry!

## The Use of Vivisection Increases

The geographic focus of vivisection shifted from Europe to the United States by 1900. A rapid increase in animal experimentation occurred towards the end of World War II and right afterwards. During the war, scientists used animals to study the effects of explosives, rapid decompression, and the treatment of wounds, as well as in their search for cures for diseases killing soldiers. To give just one example, dogs' stomachs were laid open for study. Some would survive for years until death rescued them from their miseries. An elaborate device was used to hold a dog while metal coils were inserted into its abdomen to study its reaction to various liquids.

You would think that by the 1940s our society would have enacted laws restricting animal experiments. To our shame, that is not true. There was not one piece of legislation, state or national, that prevented or mitigated the practice of vivisection. Although the battle against vivisection was old, it had not been successful. Henry Bergh, the organizer of the first Society for the Prevention of Cruelty to Animals, introduced the first American measure against vivisection in the New York legislature in January 1880. Bill after bill was introduced in Congress but none passed.

My late husband, James P. Briggs, worked long and hard to have legislation passed to outlaw all vivisection practices. As president of the National Society for the Humane Regulation of Vivisection, he called for public committee hearings to bring out evidence "that the vivisection of dogs is needlessly cruel, and serves no possible useful purpose." He started with the rescuing of dogs first because he said, "if for no other reason than dogs are the most deserving of our love and help."

At that time, pounds throughout the country were turning over unclaimed dogs for a small sum to be used in animal experiments. There was also a black market in stolen dogs. More than one pet owner lost the dog they loved and cared for to the dissecting table. Why were dogs so very valuable to the researchers? Scientists using vivisection believed that only the monkey had reactions more like humans than the dog. By reactions, they meant the way animals responded to sheer torture.

Unfortunately, sale or seizure of animals in pounds for use in laboratories are practices that continue today. For years, the National Humane Education Society has joined in the public outcry against this unspeakable—yet frequently legal—procedure.

After World War II, Government research institutions and foundations were established and expanded to promote and support clinical and animal-based biomedical research. More people were attending universities, receiving doctorates, becoming involved in research, and publishing more scientific papers and journals. Public charities were founded to support research to find cures for diseases, injuries, and birth defects. College professors involved in research were pressured to "publish or perish" as colleges received Government grants and funding for research.

The shocking result? Eighty-five percent of *all* experiments on animals have been done since 1950. What a tragic commentary on the *true* state of our supposedly enlightened society!

As experiments increased, animals were bred for laboratory use and supply companies were started. The exploitation of laboratory animals has now become big business—eight to ten billion dollars and almost 60 million animals a year!

Animals are used in several different general categories: biomedical research, development of new pharmaceuticals, toxicity testing, testing of biological compounds, educational demonstrations, and diagnosis of diseases.

Although legislation has been passed to establish humane standards for treatment of certain animals by laboratories and animal dealers, including the landmark Laboratory Animal Welfare Act in 1966, abuse and neglect are still common in laboratories. Medical schools in the United States have routinely used animals as part of the basic curriculum in teaching physiology, pharmacology, biochemistry, and surgery. In teaching labs, cruel treatment often occurs due to a lack of knowledge (the wrong nerve severed) or insensitivity (not caring for the animals properly so that they die or suffer for lack of proper food and water). Also, improperly trained students may not use the correct amount of anesthesia. Too little anesthesia allows animals to feel pain or wake up during surgery. Too much can cause death.

Another area of cruelty in education is science fair projects. Often, these are done with little supervision and no training in the proper techniques for the care and use of laboratory animals. Innocent students may not know that they are inflicting cruelty upon animals, but it is not uncommon to find school projects involving poisoning, extremely deficient diets, surgical mutilations, and deliberate torture of animals.

Surely we can educate our promising young people without tormenting helpless animals!

## *Animal Experiments—All in the Name of Science*

I shudder even to think about the experiments done on animals in the name of science and progress, but I must make myself write about it, in the hopes that others will share my outrage, and that together we will be able to put an end to vivisection in all its forms.

One of the best-known experiments is the LD50 (lethal dose 50 percent) short-term acute toxicity test. With this test, animals are injected with or forced to swallow toxic fluids such as floor polish or other cleaning products to see what amount it takes to kill them or make them ill. Or they might be forced to breathe toxic fumes to see how long they can live while inhaling measured amounts of the poisonous material. At no time during these tests are animals given any anesthesia or pain relievers. It might interfere with the results!

Read the warning labels of your household cleaners: "eye irritant," "harmful if swallowed," "keep away from children," etc. Think of the monkeys, rabbits, or mice who were blinded, burned, or killed so that warning could be placed on your container! These tests are routine for new products *and* for any change in a product's formula. That means every time you purchase a "new, improved" version of an old favorite, the LD50 test has most likely been done all over again, even if the change in the product was very minor.

Companies commission this testing to protect themselves against legal liability, should the product cause harm to humans. But is this really necessary? Don't we know by now that most cleaning agents strong enough to clean our houses may damage a part of the body as sensitive as the eye? Burn or irritate our skin? And certainly, we should have learned by now that only food products should be ingested! How many times must these experiments be repeated? How many innocent animals must suffer and die before we stop this kind of activity?

Cosmetics are also rigorously—and redundantly—tested. The LD50 test is standard in the cosmetics industry, too. For example, to see how toxic a cosmetic such as lipstick is, a cosmetic company would order a study in which large quantities of it are force-fed to animals, usually mice or rats, until 50 percent of them die. Only when half the animals are dead can the experiment be considered complete!

Another horrible experiment, the Draize Eye Test, is the most commonly used eye irritant test for cosmetic purposes. Rabbits are used for this test because the structure of their tear ducts does not allow them to rid themselves of substances placed in their eyes. Products such as hairsprays, shampoos, and conditioners are sprayed or dripped into the eyes of conscious rabbits. Of course, the rabbits have to be restrained in stocks. To measure the amount of damage done to the eyes, the tests can continue for up to seven days.

Skin irritation tests are used to test such cosmetics as deodorant, face cream, or lotion. The substance is applied directly on the shaved skin of guinea pigs or rabbits. It's left for a period of time to see what kind of reaction occurs, such as a burn or rash.

Is our vanity worth that pain? I don't think so! And apparently many women agree with me: Several new, humane-thinking companies who do not test their products on animals are doing a brisk business with sensitive, informed consumers! But these companies are still by far in the minority.

## The 21st-Century Chamber of Horrors

Experimental psychology is one area of vivisection that many researchers, veterinarians, and doctors consider to be the worst. Torture is the word that comes to mind. Animals are starved, mutilated, dehydrated, and exposed to heat, cold, electric shock, and forced aggression. Imagine a baby monkey harnessed to his surrogate mother with eyelids sewn shut and bandaged so he couldn't see.

Or envision a dog, once a family pet, placed in a metal chamber. A severe electric shock is administered. The dog jumps to the other side to avoid it, but receives an equally severe shock there. It goes back and forth until it gives up and collapses.

And that is how "learned helplessness" is demonstrated.

Then there are the terrible "living heads" experiments. In just one instance of this inconceivably barbaric exercise, two monkeys were decapitated. The head of each was grafted onto the other's body. They had no control over the bodies onto which their heads were grafted. The researchers didn't have the knowledge or didn't care enough to connect the nerves and other parts necessary to provide control. The monkeys salivated and their eyes moved, tracking the researchers. For four days, these monkeys, God's creatures just like you and me, were kept alive without anesthetic. Mercifully, they were then allowed to die.

Animals are also studied for drug/alcohol addiction. They are given drugs or alcohol, tested for the level at which they become tolerant, and turned into addicts. They are then taken off the drugs or alcohol "cold turkey" and left to suffer through the agony of withdrawal.

For years, a cigarette-smoking experiment using dogs showed researchers that the breathing rate after inhaling cigarette smoke is controlled by the vagus nerve. This nerve was surgically removed from the dogs' bodies and repositioned. That way researchers could study it better. It was found that many of the dogs would then vomit when they were forced to smoke.

Remember, many of these experiments are being paid for with your tax dollars! The grants for the dog smoking experiments came to a sum total of $387,271, but because one of the grants was renewed 26 times, it ended up costing taxpayers over $4,729,114.

And just when we think we've heard it all, the field of genetic engineering gives us something right out of a science fiction movie to ponder. These products of science offer the world a potentially endless variety of mutant creatures, unnatural beings whose lives may be a living hell. One product of engineering is a "geep" who is half sheep and half goat. "Super cows," who produce leaner meat and more milk, are being developed, and "super pigs" are being implanted with human growth hormones. A pig that was implanted with cow genes has successfully reproduced. However, its offspring has trouble walking on short legs swollen by arthritis. And it has trouble seeing because it has a severely wrinkled face and crossed eyes.

There are many troubling questions about the ethics of genetic engineering. Will it pave the way for more potentially cruel animal experiments? Is this an opening for ecological imbalance if mutant animals are released into the environment? What will happen to small farmers who can't afford this new technology? Can veterinarians keep pace with the new health

problems that are likely to develop with these new
mutations? What restrictions can be applied to prevent big businesses from monopolizing genetic stock?

The invention of a sterile oyster whose inventors
applied for a patent has caused an uproar. The patent
was granted and the doors are opened for new forms
of nonhuman animals to be developed. Heaven only
knows when genetic engineering will turn its attention
to human subjects, and where this perversion of science will ultimately lead.

## Are Animal Experiments Really Useful and Necessary?

A common belief among scientists, the media,
and many in the public is that no medical break-
through is possible without experimenting on animals.

But is it possible that the necessity and usefulness
of experimentation on animals for medical research is
exaggerated? The unqualified answer is "yes." In looking back over the history of modern medical advances,
most of these breakthroughs were made from clinical
observations of human patients. The experiments using
animals were often done to convince clinicians that the
tests should be allowed in man.

Biochemical differences between human and animal tissues are great, and often render animal-based
experimental results meaningless. For example,
dozens of human studies had shown that cigarette
smoking caused cancer prior to 1963. But, because of
outdated Government policy, warnings to the public
were delayed because for years researchers had been

trying to induce cancer in laboratory mice. It has been only recently that the medical research community recognized that while cancer induced in rodents may in some ways be fundamentally the same as that in humans, because of their differences, it may act very differently in human cells. The National Cancer Institute now tests the potential of anti-cancer agents on human cells.

The artificial heart provided another example of the limitations of animal testing. In extensive studies, the device was implanted in calves. It worked reasonably well in the animals, but when the plastic heart was placed in humans, infections, bleeding, and other complications occurred.

As with many other diseases, the greatest advances in heart research were made through studies of human patients. The same is true of efforts to control diabetes. The discovery of insulin is credited to experiments on dogs, but the hard scientific facts actually came from autopsy studies of humans.

Insufficient, unreliable, and expensive animal research continues to dominate the medical field. History shows that animal experiments are not an important part of the scientific research process but are really a sales tool to dramatize the theories arrived at from clinical research on humans.

Human diseases can't be duplicated in animals just by transmitting toxins or cells from one species to another by exposing the animals to irritating or stressful stimuli. Animals are different from humans biomechanically, biochemically, and emotionally. Consider these dramatic differences between species:

• Penicillin can be life-saving to humans but kills guinea pigs.

• Aspirin relieves pain and discomfort in humans but is fatal to cats.

• Humans have gall bladders; rats do not.

• Rats can synthesize their own vitamin C; humans cannot.

Cause and effect can be easily confused in clinical observations of animals and humans. Most scientists working in laboratories work with animal models only, not humans. They are trying to recreate a disease or medical problem in an animal which they have not studied in a human.

## How Do People Respond to Vivisection?

As with any great instance of cruelty, people react differently to the horror that is vivisection. Some turn their heads. Others purport to believe that non-human animals can't feel pain like humans do. Many just shrug their shoulders sadly. Others take a firm stand that medical research on animals is absolutely necessary, that it is the only way to find cures for human diseases and to improve the quality of life— *human* life, that is.

At the opposite end of the spectrum are those who believe that animal experimentation is morally and ethically wrong. Certainly, most would agree that animals should be used in experiments only when it is essential, and that these few should be treated kindly and humanely.

As for me, I believe that *no* animal should be

subjected to painful, usually fatal experiments—under *any* circumstances, for any reason. I respect life in all its forms, and I hope someday a majority of caring people will rise up with me to end the scourge of vivisection.

Many courageous people have already put their careers on the line to take this stand.

## Those Who've Said, "Enough Is Enough!"

Many in our society believe that animal experimentation is critical to the medical research necessary to fight disease and save the human race. Researchers using animals must feel this way; however, more and more of these scientists are beginning to question the necessity and validity of surgery and induced diseases and conditions on live animals. They're beginning to protest against some of the experiments and treatment of the animals. Some are actually leaving the research field altogether, claiming that the medical and scientific information gathered from these experiments does not benefit human life—and does not justify maiming and killing millions of innocent, defenseless animals.

The story of one caring person exemplifies this trend. A physiological psychologist with the U.S. Air Force who left the medical research field, Donald Barnes spoke out in the June 1989 issue of *The Animals' Voice Magazine*. He told of spending 18 years "vivisecting nonhuman animals for the United States Air Force." His experiments required "the pulse gamma neutron radiation (nuclear explosions) of rhesus and other monkeys," to observe the effects, and project what would happen to humans under the same conditions.

The animals were forced to fast as long as 24 hours before the irradiation procedure. They were then placed into restraint chairs. A technician administered enough radiation at the mid-brain level to kill some immediately. Others died from radiation poisoning, wasting away with bloody diarrhea and vomiting. When one monkey died, another would be ordered from the supplier. If the monkeys survived, they were to be taught to perform complex tasks while receiving shock reinforcement.

Donald Barnes did his job, continuing these types of experiments until he reached his limit. One day, he refused to take part in an experiment which he considered to be scientifically invalid. He was fired. Later, he was reinstated. He promised himself that he would do only those experiments on animals which could be proven to be beneficial to humans. When this couldn't be done, he quit.

Looking back over his years of research, he concluded that all research using live animals should be halted immediately! He is now actively involved with animal rights organizations trying to stop the pain, suffering, and death he had once had a part in causing—all in the name of science.

John McArdle was a graduate student at a major research university who eventually left academia and became involved with the animal protection movement. His story is also shared in *The Animals' Voice Magazine*. One of his first assignments was assisting another graduate student in performing brain surgery on rhesus monkeys. Neither one had any formal surgical training or had received instructions or standards on animal welfare. His concern grew for the animals' well-being.

It became morally troubling. He couldn't become an outspoken critic and still receive his Ph.D. Once he did complain about a fellow student who allowed his animals to die from sheer neglect. But the professor in charge of the project told him not to worry, that the student would learn his lesson after he had to repeat the experiments several times—because he let the animals die! This shocking lack of concern for the animals dying from neglect was evidenced on another occasion, when a department member decided to suspend an experiment using guinea pigs. He had the guinea pigs killed. Later, the experiment was rescheduled and more guinea pigs had to be ordered.

Dr. McArdle tried incorporating animal protection ethics in his teaching. Feeling threatened by the overwhelmingly inhumane research establishment, he left the teaching profession. Since then, he has been working with several animal rights organizations. Today, he is learning of more and more scientific professionals who disagree with the animal exploitation in the laboratories.

## Alternatives

Alternatives to vivisection are proving to be more accurate, less costly, and able to provide results faster—not to mention immeasurably more humane! Let's look at some of them.

Computers can be used to predict the course of a disease, or how effective a drug may be. Computer, mechanical, and mathematical models can simulate many physiological systems. For example, the analysis of body fluids and gas chromatography have proved to be cheaper and more accurate than animal testing.

Another proven alternative to vivisection is *in vitro* testing. *In vitro* research methods use tissue, cell, and organ cultures, as well as bacteria and other microorganisms which can be taken from animals and humans harmlessly. Many scientists believe *in vitro* tests are more sensitive and accurate than animal tests. Enzymes, artificial membranes, and robots can also be effective alternatives.

And modern research techniques such as CAT scans, PET scans, and magnetic imaging provide safe, ethical studies of human medical problems, while computer banks and networks can make research data instantly available to researchers, thus preventing much unnecessary duplication of experiments sharing the same methodologies and aims.

Animal rights activists also stress that the key to better human health is preventive health care. The number of people saved through prevention is much greater than those saved through medical research. In analyzing the data on the ten leading causes of death in the United States, the Centers for Disease Control found that the major factors in determining one's state of health were lifestyle, environment, heredity, and medical intervention. Another study concluded that less than four percent of Americans' increased life span since the turn of the century could be attributed to medical intervention!

In the classroom, modern methods of teaching and demonstration should be adopted that do not involve the abuse of animals. Medical and veterinary students opposed to dissection, surgery, or demonstration techniques that involve abuses or neglect to animals have spoken out on behalf of the innocent creatures penned in laboratory cages. Many find vivisection to be in direct opposition to the doctor's Hippocratic oath. Teaching methods that require hurting or killing animals in order to learn how to heal them are profoundly absurd—and unspeakably cruel!

\* \* \* \*

Haven't enough animals been drowned, shocked, burned, starved, deprived, blinded, deafened, maimed, cut, and poisoned—all in the name of science? Here at the National Humane Education Society, we believe the dark age of vivisection should be ended. And with the help of kind-hearted supporters across the country, we hope to bring about the dawning of a new age of kindness to all of God's creatures.

I've been trying to bring about that new age since I was 14 years old. It's a dream I'll never stop striving for!

# CHAPTER 3

# One Bright Spot in My Life

Often, when my work on behalf of animals has thrown a spotlight in my direction, I have been asked *why* . . . why I came to love animals so very much, and why I have devoted most of my life to doing what I could to help them. I can never answer these questions easily, because the answer seems so obvious to me: Because I love animals, I cannot stand idly by while they suffer.

But there's more to it than that. I think I have a special understanding of how animals feel when they are lost, abandoned, or neglected. For—while I was never really mistreated—I knew abandonment, loneliness, and despair as a child. Though my life since then has contained much joy, I don't think I shall ever forget the sadness of my childhood. And I know I will always want to do whatever I can to prevent others from experiencing those emotions.

Please do not think that I was not loved, or that anyone was cruel to me. Far from it—but circumstances beyond anyone's control overwhelmed our family early on. My father died when I was three, leaving my mother with four children to support on her meager wages from a Government job. She struggled to keep the family together, but finally she took the advice of relatives and placed us in orphanages.

My sister, Margaret, and I were sent to St. Vincent's Orphanage in Washington, D.C., our home town. But though we were just a few miles from home, we were petrified with fear. The terror I felt on my first night there is still clear in my mind these many years later. Looking around, we saw a huge building with many corridors *and* 150 girls of all ages. It was confusing, strange, and—that first night—a cold and unfriendly place.

Like many a lost puppy or homesick kitten, all we wanted in the world was to go home to Mother. But we could not. And when the Sisters put Margaret in a separate dormitory for older girls, I screamed so loud and so long that the Sister in charge finally had to allow my sister to come and keep me company for the night. It was the only way anyone could hope to get some sleep!

Young people today might wonder what it was like to live in an orphanage. In St. Vincent's, the orphan's life was not a bad one. Regimented, yes: Bells rang and we formed lines; obedience was firmly demanded. We had to make our own beds and perform various duties. We kept the corridors waxed and shining, every piece of furniture dusted, and all the clothes mended. It was hard work; still, we thrived. The food we ate, though bland, was nourishing and wholesome. And even though we missed our family members and our home, the Sisters were good to us.

But I can remember the days when the halls were full of whispers that someone was coming to look us over for possible adoption. I did not realize that Margaret and I were not eligible, since we still had our mother. The prospective adoptive parent would arrive, and we would all be lined up in the playroom.

I'm sure each girl hoped fervently, as I did, that she would be chosen! In our lonely children's hearts, the hope of a real home still lived on . . . the hope of our own loving family. But I was never chosen. Each time I was passed over, I was despondent.

I wonder if this is how dogs and cats feel, penned up in small cages in animal shelters, longing for their home, watching a friendly human being walk by, hoping without words for the love every animal thrives on.

At least we human orphans were not threatened with impending death when we were not chosen for adoption!

But however lonely I might have felt at the orphanage, I was soon to know an even less pleasant reality. After Margaret and I had spent several years at St. Vincent's, Mother decided to bring Margaret home. For some reason, she sent me to live with an aunt and uncle in Frederick, Maryland. The separation from my sister puzzled and hurt me. But in those days you did not question your parents; you did as you were told. I had no choice: Off to Frederick, Maryland I went.

There I was enlisted to do all the chores for the

household. In those days, there were few modern conveniences, so housework was long and laborious. Having been well trained at the orphanage, I took up my tasks without hesitation. There was not a moment of time to spare for playing at home. Worse yet, I was told that I could not even play at recess at school . . . because my aunt forbade me to get my dress dirty!

Soon I was given additional duties: I became responsible for the entire family's laundry. Remember, there were no washing machines or dryers in those days, no drip-dry clothes, nothing to make the task quicker or easier. I knew many a tired and discouraged moment before the age of 12, leaning over a washboard, feeling very alone.

In the summer, my aunt—like most country people of that era—did an enormous amount of canning. So I spent my summer days washing Mason jars and preparing fruits and vegetables. Bushels and bushels of beans, tomatoes, peas, squash, peaches, and apples passed through my young fingers. And *then* there were the jellies and preserves!

For the four years I lived at my aunt's, I could not even enjoy the simple pleasure of reading. Though her stepson had a few interesting-looking books in the bookshelf—including some Horatio Alger volumes—I was told to read only the *Bible* or *Pilgrim's Progress.* Before this edict was handed down, I had a chance to read one of the Alger books. Then I was told that such books were not suitable reading for girls, and I was forbidden to touch them.

But the rags-to-riches, action-filled Alger stories were tempting to a curious child. Taking pity on me, one of my friends at school brought me an Alger book to read there. But one day the teacher caught me reading it, instead of my textbook. I was soundly scolded. Worse yet, Miss Rinehart reported my crime to my aunt the next Sunday morning after church. My aunt glared at me as only she could, and I burst into tears.

I was lucky that day, however. Our pastor, Mr. Royal, overheard my outburst and asked me what was wrong. I was crying too hard to speak, so my aunt explained my grievous misbehavior. To his everlasting credit, Mr. Royal defended me.

"I should think Miss Rinehart could do better things at church than tattle on a little girl who wasn't doing any harm," he said firmly. My aunt never gave me the punishment I'm sure I would have received had not Mr. Royal—the father of two young girls himself—intervened.

Truly, there is no end to the fantasies an unhappy child can create! From that day forward, I dreamed that Mr. Royal was my father, and that his daughters were my sisters. I got through my gruelling household chores by pretending I was doing them for my *own* family, the Royal family.

These were the darkest days of my childhood. I longed for my mother and sister. I longed for play, and for playmates. My aunt forbade me even to play with dogs. She said she had been mauled as a child. Therefore, she said I must cross the street if I saw one. Not knowing dogs, I had no choice but to obey.

When I think today of the many thousands of wonderful dogs who have given me joy, I only wish I could have had a dog friend in those sad, lonely years.

Those years with my aunt stand out in memory as years of isolation and yearning, hard work and little reward for a child so young. I am sure my aunt never meant to mistreat me, but she certainly saw my role more as servant than as family member.

Try as she might, however, my aunt could not suppress all the joy in my life. She kept a canary in a cage in her parlor. The beautiful bird sang and chirped happily, keeping me company on my household rounds. When my aunt took her nap, I stole the time to talk to him for a few moments. I loved taking care of him—cleaning his cage, feeding him, and fixing his bath.

As has been true so many times in my life, in those years an animal gave me the gifts of love, pleasure, and companionship. That little canary was the one bright spot in my life—a spirit-restoring presence in a sad little girl's days.

Today, when I have an opportunity to do something for an animal, I think of that canary, and I'm grateful to be able to return the favor.

I only wish more animals were free to share their sweet companionship in good health and good spirits, as God so clearly intended them to do!

# CHAPTER 4

# Carnival or Carnage: Animals in Entertainment

*"The greatness of a nation and its moral progress can be measured by the way its animals are treated."*

—Mahatma Gandhi

In my years of animal welfare work, I've tried to help many a terrified and mistreated creature. For me, there is always an anger that wells up at the thought of people being cruel to innocent animals. It's simply not something I can understand. And I find it particularly hard to grasp why some people find the mistreatment of animals amusing, funny, or diverting.

But they certainly do. In circuses, in rodeos, in bullfights. In trained animal acts everywhere. In dog racing and horse racing.

At Peace Plantation, we have had the good fortune to be able to rescue several horses from severe mistreatment. One of them, Lollipop, a beautiful chestnut mare, had been what was known as a Tennessee walking horse, trained to walk in a strange, unnatural gait that could only have been stressful and painful to the animal. Gradually, Lollipop realized that she would never have to perform this way for us, and I know she was glad. I puzzled often over this question: When the animal's own way of moving is so beautiful, so graceful, why in the world would anybody want to pervert it in this way, to fit their own strange idea of attractiveness?

Of course I've never figured out an answer to that question—or to the question of why cruelty is called entertainment in the case of a shameful spectacle known as a bullfight.

## *"Corrida de Toros":* Torture as National Sport

We humans have used animals to amuse and entertain us for centuries. Most of these creatures have been unwilling participants in our games. Many have paid dearly with their lives or through extreme suffering. How did this begin? Bullfighting, circuses, rodeos, animal races, and other so-called games, many of them pitting man against animal, had their origins in early Greek, Roman, and Spanish civilizations.

Though all of these "entertainments" subject animals to unspeakable mistreatment, the bullfight, in which many other animal-based entertainments had their start, is perhaps the most chilling—simply because it has been so thoroughly glamorized, and even elevated to the status of an art form in some people's eyes!

How did this deadly game begin? Sadly, it is an ancient tradition. "Corrida de toros," meaning to run the bulls, has been the national sport of Spain for hundreds of years. As far back as 228 B.C., there were tales of games using bulls in the Spanish province of Andalusia, where men showed their dexterity and bravery, then dealt the blow of death to "the savage horned beast" with an ax or lance. Although many people think we have become much more civilized and enlightened during the past few centuries, the sad plight of the bull hasn't changed.

Julius Caesar brought this new form of spectacle with bulls to Rome. Previously, Romans had used a more domesticated cattle in their entertainment. The Iberian stock was wilder, more spirited. Iberians would use skins or cloaks to avoid the bulls' attacks, then kill them. The first Roman amphitheater, "Statilus Taurus," was built for the Roman nobles and other Roman citizens to enjoy this "heroic" display of man and beast. Spectators watching this "entertainment" could be sure of a kill—of either the bull or the man sentenced to meet the bull, usually criminals or those who didn't profess the religion of the state.

Bullfighting evolved through the years. In Spain, bull-lancing tournaments were the favorite sport of the aristocracy. Picadors, peons on horseback, were used. Bull breeding became financially profitable by the 1700s. The royal houses in Spain, France, Portugal, Italy, and even the Catholic Church in Spain had representatives competing in the ring. Short barbed darts and dogs of prey were used to worry the bull and make it more spirited. The dogs were specially bred so that their nostrils and protruding underjaw permitted them to breathe while hanging on to the bull.

Papal threats of excommunication brought a radical change to the "bull joust." The nobles were forced to give up their roles in the ring to professional subordinates of a lower social class. These replacements traded the lance for the sword which is still used to kill the bull in bullfights today.

Bullfighting became a very popular "sport." Today, Spain has over 250 "plazas de toros" (bull rings) of all sizes, accommodating crowds from one thousand to many thousands. Mexico City has a huge "plaza de toros" and there are numbers of them throughout Latin America.

Six bulls are usually killed during one bullfight. Just imagine six times 250. That would be at least 1,500 bulls killed if each bull ring in Spain held just one bullfight! Think of the magnitude of the slaughter worldwide and over a period of time! And think, too, of the unnecessary suffering and torment the bulls are subjected to, all in the name of entertainment.

The bulls used for bullfighting are of a pedigreed lineage bred on special ranches. Soon after the year-ling males are weaned, vaccinated, and branded, they are tested in the open field to see if they are spirited enough to fight. Those of outstanding pedigree, true coloration, and very fine physical build are separated from the others. At three years of age, these chosen animals are put through stud tests to prove they have the proper spirit. If they pass these tests, they are kept to be used exclusively at stud for about 15 years. If they fail, they are sent to the slaughterhouse.

Heifers are tested at two to three years of age in a small ring on the ranch through all phases of the "corrida." Those who pass will be used for breeding. Those who don't are slaughtered.

Bulls are never used the second time in a bull-fight. Their memories are quite good. They must be totally innocent of the bull ring in order to be appropriate opponents—or victims—for the matador.

The color red was chosen for the work cape used by the matador and his assistants to minimize the sight of blood and other stains. Also, the red cape helps stage a more colorful production. The red cape means nothing to the bull: Bulls are color blind, as are all cattle.

The professional bull fighters are: the matadors, the main performers; their assistants, the banderillos, who also work on foot, use a cape and pierce the bull with short, barbed darts called banderillas; and the picadors, who ride on horses using pike-poles.

Each bullfight begins with a grand procession into the ring of the matadors' troupes with the mule teams, used to drag out the carcasses of the bulls, bringing up the rear. Typically, after the procession, the town's mayor throws down the key to the bull pens. The door is opened. As the bull passes through, an attendant situated above attaches a silken rosette of the bull's ranch's colors into the shoulder muscles of the bull.

The banderillos attract the bull's attention and draw his attack with the cape to allow the matador time to judge whether the bull shows a preference of charging with one horn or both. A bugle call is sounded within ten seconds and the matador begins his performance with the silken work cape. The picadors enter at a second bugle call. When the bull sees the horse, he charges it and the picador must fend off the bull's attack with his pike-pole, planting the point right between the neck and shoulder blades.

The horses, too, are victims in the bullfight, vulnerable to horrible disembowelment by the charging bull. A protective armor of compressed cotton encased in leather and canvas is now used to shield the horse's belly. This has helped to alleviate much of the harm to the horses, but the armor is not impenetrable. The matadors then perform. Another bugle call is sounded as the banderillos precisely plant two to four pairs of the short barbed darts; these make the bull lose preference for attack with either horn so he may attack equally, making it a well-rounded performance!

Now the "Hour of Truth" dawns. The matador is alone. His assistants are present only in an emergency or when requested.

The matador takes his place below the mayor's box and asks permission to dedicate the bull to someone to whom he tosses his hat. He gracefully performs and proves his mastery over the bull. At no time is the matador allowed to touch the bull except for the kill.

When that dreadful time comes, the matador thrusts his cape forward with one hand, causing the bull to lower his head for attack. With the other hand, the matador sinks the sword into the bull's shoulder blades at the junction of the neck. The blade of the sword should cut through diagonally, severing the aorta and causing almost instant death. If done well, there should be no blood. If blood appears, it is usually because the lungs were pierced, which is not considered good form. More than one thrust of the sword is allowed if the proper procedures are followed.

After the kill, the matador and his assistants circle the arena in victory. The matador returns for his hat which is usually returned to him with money or gifts.

If the performance has been excellent, the matador receives one ear of the bull. If it has been exceptional, he receives two ears. However, if it has been highly superior, he receives both ears and the tail.

What sickening trophies! I wonder what kind of person could possibly want these sad reminders of a once-majestic animal, bullied, tortured, and trapped, then brutally killed? For such an act of ignominy, severed body parts are too good a reward!

While the matador is receiving acclaim, an attendant with a short blade severs the bulls' spinal cord at the base of his skull and the bull's carcass, quartered and dressed, is dragged from the arena.

Thus concludes the so-called pageantry of the bullfight, a travesty created not of art or skill but of cruelty and violence.

On an encouraging note, attendance at bullfights has been declining since 1987. Recent Spanish newspaper polls show that 50 percent of citizens polled no longer have an interest in bullfighting. Members of the British and West German Parliaments have put forward a proposal to ban bullfighting in the European community. The proposal would also ban other events involving animals, such as dog- and cock-fighting and fox-hunting. Spanish animal rights groups are supporting this proposal.

Traditions die slowly, but perhaps this is the beginning of the end of the cruel "sport" of bullfighting. Maybe one day, horses and bulls will no longer have to be the unwilling victims in bullfights—one of man's most vicious entertainments.

And perhaps in America we'll ban our own cruel games, like the rodeo, our very own, home-grown form of the bullfight!

## Rodeos, Circuses, and Races: They're Not Fun for the Animals!

Rodeos are a series of cowboy contests. Usually, they consist of events such as saddle bronco riding, bareback riding, calf roping, bull riding, steer wrestling, and team roping.

These events grew out of contests between men working in the early cattle industry. Often, these men would be forced to spend months and even years on the range in the southwestern part of the United States. These contests were a way to entertain themselves. Today, the rodeo has grown into big-business entertainment around the world.

Rodeo animals are quite valuable. The horses and steers are good, strong stock. Good bucking horses are not from wild herds but are usually gentle until mounted and halter-broken. These horses are encouraged to dislike being mounted. A flank strap placed around the hindquarters makes them have a tendency to buck, as any foreign object on the rear of a horse will do.

For the most part, the animals are well cared for to ensure the best performance and competition in the arena. However, as amateur and professional rodeos proliferate around the world, animal care standards are deteriorating. Equipment is placed on the horses and they are goaded to do things they wouldn't ordinarily do unless aggravated. Poorly trained performers and caretakers can accidentally injure the animals as well as themselves.

And once again, animals are the unwilling participants, forced to go against their own instincts to give us something we call entertainment!

In circuses, too, animals have suffered and still do today. Wild animal acts have always been popular. People thrill at watching exotic jungle beasts jump through hoops or rings of fire at the crack of a whip. Spectators are in awe at the demonstrated power of man over beast. But the spirit of these magnificent animals has been broken forever. And often the care and treatment of the animals is far from humane. Are they treated well in training? What kind of everyday care do they receive? Dogs, horses, elephants, lions, tigers, and others are all on the move constantly in small, makeshift quarters. How are they cared for during transportation from place to place?

Dog racing is another big animal entertainment business. The Massachusetts Society for the Prevention of Cruelty to Animals reported in its magazine,

*Animals*, that "Massachusetts dog tracks held 10,596 dog races with 2,630,092 people attending" in 1986. The state collected a whopping $29,315,298 in total revenue—big business indeed!

The greyhound is the sleek racing machine that provides entertainment on the dog tracks. Known for their lithe shape, graceful stride, and fine performance, greyhounds are carefully screened before they have a chance to show their speed and grace on the tracks. Each greyhound is put through training and a series of qualifying races. At any stage in these tryouts, if the dog fails to do well, it is killed, sold, turned over to be used in biomedical research, or, occasionally, adopted as a pet.

The greyhound that makes it through the qualifying races and has a full career on the race track usually can count on a life span of about three-and-a-half years. Then the dog's racing days are considered over and the owners dispose of the animal.

Estimates place the number of greyhounds killed each year at up to 50,000. What a tragic waste of life!

Sadly, again we see people using animals for their own pleasure at a very high cost to animal life. When will human beings stop to remember that animals are God's creatures too—not just disposable byproducts to be used at man's will?

I thought I had heard just about everything there was to hear about animal abuse in entertainment. But recently I learned of another bizarre and terrible amusement. A new type of rodeo has caught on in the quiet waters of the Gulf of Mexico. It's called the "Deep Sea Fishing Rodeo." After hearing the details about this one, I think you might question along with me whether it might be more accurately referred to as a "kill tournament," deep-sea fishing taken to an unimaginable new low.

At one three-day tournament, around 2,400 sport fishermen caught 100,000 fish. Of these, most are dead when they reach the shore and the spectators don't see the fight for life that is waged or realize that fish, too, feel pain when bladders rupture and hooks pierce them.

The fishing boat came in with a prize—not one shark but three sharks—on board. Nothing brings as much excitement to a deep sea fishing rodeo or tournament as a shark hanging. The jubilant crew forces the hook of a giant crane into the lifeless shark's jaws. It is raised from the deck and suspended hanging in the air for ten minutes or more to the delight of the cheering crowd.

This scene is repeated twice. The shark corpses are left to hang and be admired by the crowd. As night settles in and the people begin to leave for home, the sharks are cut down, taken back to sea, and dumped—of no more use to man!

I'm relieved to tell you that at last some progress is being made in one area of the animal entertainment business, television and motion pictures. Yes, even though I'm sure most of us have enjoyed watching tales of the Old West with beautiful horses riding by carrying the hero, or Flipper, the lovable dolphin, or many other animal-related comedies or dramas, there is a darker side to what we see on the screen. Did you ever wonder how those animals were treated during the filming of the movie?

Sadly, severe mistreatment of animals has

occurred on film locations. For example, in a dramatic escape scene calling for a stunt man to ride his horse off a cliff, the rider survived, but the horse fell 70 feet onto rapids below and broke his back. Many other incidences of cruel treatment have been reported, involving all kinds of animals.

Rallied by tragedies like these, members of the entertainment community are calling for strict reforms. The American Humane Association also tries to monitor the use of animals in film production. A 24-hour-a-day hotline allows anyone who sees mistreatment of an animal on a movie set to call confidentially and report the abuse.

But these animals, as well as all animals involved in any form of so-called entertainment, will be safe only when market forces protect them—that is, when people no longer rush to pay to see degrading, dangerous animal acts, to participate in such horrors as the Deep Sea Rodeo, and to cheer on the bloodthirsty matador. We must abstain from these deadly pastimes, and we must sustain a public outcry against all such abuses.

At the National Humane Education Society, we need your help to educate and encourage people to open their eyes and see these activities for what they really are.

Legislation must be passed to protect these animals from slaughter, from injury, and pain. If God has entrusted to us the care of His creatures, we must exercise our duties with love and kindness. Let us be entertained by the carnival of nature in its natural state, not by the unnatural carnage of animals sacrificed for the momentary pleasure of man.

# CHAPTER 5

# Tut, Sport, and a Man Called Briggsie

If you, dear reader, are an animal-lover as I am, you will understand why I am so determined to spare animals unnecessary pain. And you will also understand why I sometimes say my life really began only after I returned from my aunt's home in Frederick, Maryland, and I began to get to know some animals first-hand.

Though I did not like to complain, I reached a turning point just after my thirteenth birthday, in early December of 1922. I wrote to Mother asking her to send me the train fare to come home for Christmas. I asked her, too, if there was any way I could return home permanently. I was so unhappy, so lonely, and yet I had never had an opportunity to tell Mother this when she visited me in Frederick. Somehow she scraped together the train fare, and I had my chance at last.

I will never forget stepping off the train at Washington's Union Station and into the arms of my sister, Margaret, and my brother, Jack. How happy I was to see them! At last, I felt free—for the first time in my life. The three of us celebrated with a chocolate sundae, bought at a delicatessen on Wisconsin Avenue. It was my first chocolate sundae ever, a wonderful treat made even more delicious by the joy of being with my brother and sister.

My family was living in a tiny, four-room house in Georgetown, now a very fancy neighborhood, but then just a working-class, down-to-earth place. My coming home meant that Margaret and Mother would have to share their bedroom with me. I was grateful that they seemed to do so willingly. Now I had to adjust to having no electricity and no central heating, luxuries I had known at the orphanage and at my aunt's house. But these were small deprivations in my mind. At last I was home!

Best of all, though, at last I got to know a dog— a five-week-old puppy named Tut, given to my sister, Margaret. Because Margaret worked as an addressograph operator, it was my job to care for Tut before and after school. A world of pure joy opened up to me! The puppy and I spent every available moment together. Caring for Tut was not a chore to me, but an endless delight.

When I looked into Tut's warm brown eyes, when I played with her, when I stroked her smooth, warm coat, I could only think how very, very wrong my aunt had been about dogs!

But this paradise could not last. Six months

after we got Tut, my mother decided she could not let me keep her because she was a female. I had no idea what the implications of being female were, and why that would mean that Tut would have to go — but once again, there was no arguing with one's mother in those days. At the time, neither Mother nor I knew about spaying. To Mother, there was no alternative, but I was crushed at the idea of having to give Tut away.

I asked every friend and acquaintance if they could take Tut, but no one could. I decided to take her to the delicatessen where I had enjoyed my first ice cream sundae. There I stood on the street with Tut in my arms, asking passersby if they could give my dog a home. It took everything in me to offer Tut over to other people—people I didn't even know! But it had to be done.

At last, two young men approached me. Seeing the tears stream down my face, one of them offered to take Tut. He said she could live at his office where he sold coal. I watched Tut to see how she reacted to him. They took to each other, and thus I lost my first real friend.

Heartbroken, I went home. I was devastated at the loss of Tut. Somehow, a few days later, I managed to get a nickel and I called the man who had taken her. He said she was doing fine. After that I thought it best not to call him any more.

More changes were coming. Mother had her eye on a house for sale in northeast Washington, on Capitol Hill, and she had managed to work overtime long enough to scrape together a deposit. In February

1924, we moved. Still grieving for Tut, now I had to adjust to a new school and classmates. Fortunately, Valentine's Day was just around the corner, and when Valentines were distributed, I received some from my new schoolmates. I felt much better. That was a good school year for me, with an interesting teacher and nice new friends, and gradually I recovered from the loss of Tut.

As I got to know my new neighborhood, I met many people who were out walking their dogs. One lady told me about the Animal Rescue League not too far from my new home. I thought to myself, "It *must* be a wonderful place if they have dogs!" I asked her for directions. The next Sunday afternoon, I ran most of the way there.

Leona, the lady in charge, took me to the kennels. I had never seen a kennel before. Leona told me that not every dog would find a home. I determined that I would at least give them some extra love and caring, and every Sunday after that I ran down Capitol Hill to the Animal Rescue League, where Leona let me feed, water, and play with the dogs. My life was immeasurably happier now!

I would run back home after my hours at the League, overflowing with stories about the dogs I loved so much. I was overjoyed when Mother said I could have a male terrier puppy if the League had one to give me. She believed a terrier would kill any rats that might threaten our household. I myself did not care what kind of dog we got. Any dog would be wonderful!

When I went to the League on Palm Sunday 1924, Leona told me she had a puppy for me. He was curled up in a cage, sound asleep, a wee little pup of just six weeks, all white except for a bit of tan on his ears. Leona handed him to me with a big smile. I was ecstatically happy. I managed to thank her and took my precious ball of fur to show Mother. I named him "Sport," and with his presence in my life, the pain remaining from Tut's loss truly began to fade from my heart and mind.

I no longer had time to grieve over Tut, since Sport demanded a lot of care. He was very good at night, but as the sun rose, he would whimper—lonely for his mother and his littermates, no doubt. I would race downstairs and hold him until Mother got up at 6 a.m. Then I fed Sport and took him for a walk, taking tiny short steps so as not to hurry him. When I left for school, he settled down for a nap. I raced home during lunch time to feed him and take him out for his constitutional. He slept again in the afternoon, and after school he stayed in the yard until after the evening meal. We fed Sport table scraps. It didn't take much to fill him up since he was so tiny.

As Sport grew, it became clear that he was not going to kill rats as Mother had hoped. One day, I fed Sport outside, then watched him let a rat come right up and eat his food. Wisely, I thought, Sport had decided to give the rat plenty of room! Rats were not his enemies. He might have even thought of them as friends! I decided to feed Sport inside the house only from then on, but the rats kept coming, as if they expected something. I fed them leftover bread. To me, they were animals like any others. But you can imagine how Mother felt when she found out! She promptly put a stop to my rat-feeding.

Soon Mother decided Sport was not fulfilling his duties as expected. Now a medium-sized dog, Sport obviously had no intention of killing anything. The handwriting was on the wall: Sport was going to have to go. When Mother handed down this decision, I wanted to run away with my dog, but my common sense prevailed. I went to Leona at the Animal Rescue League.

"Sport will have to be put to sleep if you bring him here," she told me. There was no way I was going to let that happen to my happy, healthy friend! So I went to see the lady who had first told me about the League.

"You know, I've heard about a farm for homeless animals," she said. "It's run by a Mr. Briggs. Why don't you telephone him?" She looked up his phone number for me. I called, my hopes high for my little dog. The lady who answered the phone said she would give Mr. Briggs my message, but he never called me.

On a very cold January day in 1925, I was talking with a neighbor in front of my house when a large collie came up to me. Icicles were clinging to the fur of this beautiful, obviously purebred dog; he bore no identification. The neighbor had never seen him before, nor had I. As we pondered what to do, a middle-aged man stopped and asked us if the dog was lost.

"I don't know, but I think so," I told him, "and we don't know what to do about him."

The kindness in the man's blue eyes was readily apparent. "I run a farm for homeless animals," he said. "I can send a man tomorrow to pick up the dog, if we can find shelter for him tonight."

I looked at him in astonishment. "You must be Mr. Briggs!" I exclaimed.

Indeed, it *was* Mr. Briggs. Already I thought he seemed like the kindest man I had ever met.

"I called your house weeks ago," I told him, "and I left you a message, and you never called back!"

It turned out that the lady who took my message was his cousin. She had a habit of not passing on messages about animals in distress, because she didn't want Mr. Briggs to bring them to the house, even though it was not her home. Now that he knew my story, Mr. Briggs would be able to help me. I was so relieved!

I took the collie home to try to keep him in our garage overnight, so Mr. Briggs could have him picked up the next day. But when the man came for the dog, the collie had managed to find a way out of the enclosure, and was gone. I explained to the driver that, though there was no collie to pick up, I had to give up my own dog, Sport, and asked him to take my pet to Mr. Briggs' farm.

When the man picked up my Sport to put him into the truck, I ran into the house to cry my eyes out. But at least I knew he would not have to be put to death.

Months went by. I wondered about Sport, about how he was doing. Once again I spent my days grieving for a dog I loved and had been forced to give up.

Eventually, I met Mr. Briggs on the street when he was out walking his own dog. I asked him about Sport, but he did not know specifically about my dog. He invited me to join a party of other ladies who visited the farm on Sundays, if my mother would give me permission. My heart leapt with joy when Mother said yes, and a trip was arranged for the next Sunday.

When we arrived at the farm, located in what was then the Maryland countryside, I jumped out of the car, wildly excited about the prospect of seeing my Sportie again. I "met" every one of the 150 dogs at the farm, but Sport was not there. The lady in charge told me that a white terrier with tan ears had been adopted by a family with two children a few months before. My heart sank because I would never see Sport again, but I was happy for my little dog. He was in good hands, and I knew it would be selfish to wish to have him back again.

That day, Mr. Briggs showed me around his 80-acre "Be Kind to Animals Rest Farm." In addition to the 150 dogs, there were 65 cats, 10 horses, and a good many cattle. I held some of the dogs while Mr. Briggs treated them for mange. Though he worked hard as an attorney during the week, Mr. Briggs loved animals so much that he devoted every spare moment to their rescue and care. I had never met anyone so generous with his love and caring before. I left the Farm with a new sense of joy in my heart. Just knowing about the Farm, and about Mr. Briggs, made me deeply happy.

My visits to the Farm became a regular occurrence. I lived for each Sunday to arrive. In 1925, I got my driver's license —a rather rare thing for a young woman in those days—and I became the regular Sunday driver of the Humane Education Society's new vehicle, a Model A sedan, almost luxurious with its heater and automatic windshield wiper.

Every Sunday, I was getting to know James P. Briggs better and better. And every Sunday, I found there was more and more to admire.

Mr. Briggs had started his organization in 1920, mortgaging his home to purchase the 80-acre property that became the "Be Kind To Animals Rest Farm." He built the Farm's animal pens mostly by himself, learning carpentry as he went along.

In addition to rescuing animals and taking them to the Farm, Mr. Briggs held public meetings to inform people about the suffering of animals in steel-jaw traps, laboratories, cruel sports and practices, roadside zoos, and farms and slaughterhouses. He struggled tirelessly to publicize the plight of animals, writing letter after letter to William Randolph Hearst, Sr., trying to get the great publisher interested in exposing the cruelty in laboratories. I helped him with this correspondence, typing some of the letters. We were so gratified when Mr. Hearst devoted the centerfold of *The American Weekly* to this important subject.

Though I had been forced to drop out of school and take a job at a dry cleaner's to help my family's finances, I was learning a lot about humane work from Mr. Briggs in those teenage years. In fact, I was forming my vocation with his help. He taught me how to get people involved, how to care for animals, how to launch an effective protest against inhumane practices. He inspired me, nurturing my childlike love for animals into an adult commitment, encouraging me to be a vegetarian, as he was.

Until then I had never heard of a vegetarian, but in practice, I had just about become one. When Sport had been with us, I realized he needed meat in addition to the table scraps we gave him. I was only too glad to give him my share, along with a lot of gravy I would make and pour over any leftovers we might have had. Nobody had ever heard of canned dog food in those days!

For Mr. Briggs, being a vegetarian followed out of his commitment to animals. He told how cattle and sheep on trains and in slaughterhouses suffered miserably. From that day on, I have never eaten flesh, and I have never missed it. Nor did my children eat meat or fish. Yet, contrary to popular belief, we were all healthy, able to out-work many of our meat-eating counterparts!

With Mr. Briggs' help, I learned how to rescue and care for animals who had been terribly mistreated, and soon I had an opportunity to test my skills on my own. In the spring of 1925, a friend told me about a next-door neighbor who was beating his German Shepherd almost daily. Apparently the man wanted the dog to act like Rin-Tin-Tin, then a popular canine matinee idol. But no amount of training, shouting, and beating made the poor dog do tricks like the man had seen on the movie screen. Though the man had named the dog "Cy"—short for "Cyclone"—there was nothing energetic about this oft-beaten, pathetic animal.

My friend told the man about me, and that I would be willing to take Cy off his hands, but the man would not relent. The poor dog was in terrible shape, afraid even to walk. This infuriated the man even more, and he whipped him mercilessly. Finally the man realized he would never win this battle with Cy, and that no one would buy him in the shape he was in. So he called my friend and said, "You tell that friend of yours she had better come and get this dog before I kill it."

When my friend called, I ran to the man's house immediately. Thinking I might hurt him, the dog shook and looked for a hiding place. My heart went out to the poor thin creature, and though he was nearly full-grown, I picked Cy up and carried him home. When I put him on the floor, he ran behind a chair and put his head under it, trying to find shelter.

Of course I knew Mother would likely be very unhappy about Cy's presence in our home. But she, too, admired Rin-Tin-Tin, and because Cy was a German Shepherd, I thought she might give him a chance. I knew I could fall back on Mr. Briggs if Mother would not relent. To my surprise, however, Mother felt sorry for Cy, even though it was obvious he was in no shape to catch any rats!

It took months to restore Cy to health, months of tender loving care I was only too glad to give. I would speak soothingly to him, kneeling on the floor if he was hiding. For a long time, Cy would not come out of his hiding place unless I coaxed him. Eventually, he would come out for my sister, but my brothers apparently reminded him forcefully of his former owner, and he stayed away from them. It took several months before Cy would accept their overtures.

By summertime, I could take Cy into the front yard, holding him and stroking him. He needed the support of my touch and constant "baby talk" in order to believe that all was well. He held his tail between his legs so much that people thought it had been cut off, so I taught him how to wag his tail again, moving it gently with my hand for five minutes at a time. Eventually he started wagging it himself, and the day came when he no longer kept it hidden between his legs. How happy that made me!

Though he still liked to hide behind his chair, Cy gradually grew bolder, happily running in the park with me. And one day, with the help of some puppies, he learned to trust Mother.

Someone had asked me to keep a couple of puppies for a few hours, which I did gladly. When Mother returned from work, and I explained that the puppies were not permanent additions to the household, she knelt down to play with them. Cy was very interested and watched Mother avidly as she petted the little puppies. Inching forward, Cy came over to investigate. Seeing that she liked the puppies, Cy realized that she might like him, too! Suddenly, the ice was broken. Mother reached down and patted Cy on the head, and Cy actually wagged his tail happily. I was thrilled!

After that day, Cy never had the shakes again. But still he had never barked. One day, though, we were both on the third floor of the house. Someone was at the door, and Cy ran downstairs barking. I followed him, delighted, and threw open the door. I shouted to the unsuspecting bread man, "My dog barked! Isn't that *great*?" I'm sure the man thought I was a lunatic. After all, what would you expect of a full-grown German Shepherd?

I explained Cy's story, and the bread man told me

that until that day he had never known we even had a
dog. Cy now had the confidence to be a watch dog! I
was thrilled, and even Mother was pleased: At last, a
dog who could pull his weight in our household!

Cy was smart, too. Though I never tried to teach
him any tricks, Cy learned to run and get his leash
whenever I combed my hair in front of the mantelpiece
mirror. When we went to the store, he seemed to want to
carry something home, so I gave him a small basket. He
would carry a lightweight item in it as we walked home
together companionably. In fact, Cy became a real
expert on grocery-buying. When he knew I was about to
go out, he would carry Mother's purse to her by the
strap. She would take out a five- or ten-dollar bill, which
Cy would carry to me. Then he would pick up his little
basket, ready to go to the store.

On our walks, Cy and I often encountered Mr.
Briggs, out walking his dog. Sometimes we would sit
together, and Mr. Briggs would confide in me about
his struggles to keep the farm going. Getting adequate
help was a constant concern; caretakers did not want
to stay at a place without central heating, electricity, or
running water. I felt so sorry for this dedicated man
who worked all day in the city, then spent every
available moment—*and* every available dollar—to
care for the animals he loved.

Though there were many years between us, Mr.
Briggs and I seemed to have a special understanding.
Certainly we had a shared commitment to helping
animals, but Mr. Briggs was equally kind to people—
especially to me, I thought. Whenever he thought of a
special pleasure I might like, he saw to it that I had the
opportunity to enjoy it, by giving me tickets to a

movie about animals, for example. My admiration for Mr. Briggs was growing into real love, and one day I let my feeling show.

We were out walking our dogs when I thought of something I had wanted to tell him. Without thinking, I blurted out, "Oh, Briggsie," the special name I called him in my mind. Embarrassed, I told him I had never intended to call him that, but he laughed and said he was glad of it.

Briggsie began to meet me almost every evening, after my shift at the dry cleaner's ended at 8:00. Though I was only 17 when he asked me to marry him, I had no doubts. I knew my family and friends would disapprove of our age difference, but we both knew in our hearts that it could be bridged—and that it already had been.

On my 18th birthday, December 9, 1927, Briggsie and I went to Ellicott City, Maryland, where we were married in a parsonage. When the ceremony was over, the pastor told us he never married anyone unless he felt they were right for one another. He confided that he was absolutely certain that we would make a good married life together.

And that we did. For the next 18 years, I knew the great happiness of being married to the kindest man I have ever met—a man who would do anything to help people or animals in need.

Today I like to think that, through our love, Briggsie and I were able to help the innocent creatures he loved so much. And it is in his memory that I continue the work we started together—work I will do with love in my heart until I am no longer able to continue it.

# CHAPTER 6

# Crimes Against Nature

There's a story I love that dates back to 1932. It's about a farmer on Maryland's Eastern Shore who loved Canada geese. He left part of his corn crop unharvested each year so the big birds would continue to come to his land as a haven in winter.

As the story goes, the farmer became very ill at age 85 and asked to spend his last days at home with his family. Children and grandchildren cried at his bedside as he lay dying. They knew the end was near, and they waited for him to awake so they could ask him a last question.

"What can we do for you, Granddad?"

He replied, "What time of year is it?"

"Thanksgiving," they said.

"Ah yes, the time when the wild geese come back. Look out the window and see if they are back in the fields."

The grandchildren looked and said, "Yes, Granddad, they are back."

"Good," he said, "something is still right in the world. The geese are still migrating. If you want to help, carry on in my behalf so the geese will always have this sanctuary."

And he closed his eyes and peacefully passed away.

The farmer's wish became a reality one year later, as the marshy wetlands near his farm were purchased by the Interior Department and set aside as a permanent, protected wildlife habitat called the Blackwater Wildlife Refuge.

I cherish this story because I experience such joy each time I return to the Blackwater Refuge. The honking of the big birds as they fly into the area is a special part of nature's music. Today, more than 50,000 wild geese, ducks, and swans winter on the refuge. The endangered bald eagle, peregrine falcon, and red-cockaded woodpecker are at home on the refuge, along with the red fox, blue herons, white-tailed deer, muskrats, raccoons, opossums, skunks, and nutria.

The Blackwater Refuge is just one of more than 450 refuges permanently set aside for wildlife throughout the United States. Administered by the U.S. Fish and Wildlife Service, more than half of them host endangered species, animals in severe and imminent danger of disappearing forever off the face of the earth.

About 350 animals are on the Interior Department's official endangered species list. We know that 75 percent of this total were hurt by destruction of their habitat caused by lumbering, fires, farming, suburban sprawl, highway construction, and dam-building across rivers and marshes. Water and air pollution and hunting also harmed these creatures.

We need more Blackwater refuges and must join together to champion wetlands acquisition and preservation, and to restore areas damaged by pollution. Halting all hunting in key marshlands will also help. We must act decisively, and soon—or there will be nothing left to protect!

How did we reach this frightening place, where our whole planet is truly endangered? Well, for millennia, the varieties of animal and plant life have been abundant on our earth. Man has hunted and killed animals for food and sport, assuming that the supply is endless. Forests have been decimated for building homes, roads, and cities. Today, as overpopulation stresses our environment more than ever, we must ask ourselves at what price our "progress" has been made.

The scientists' forecast for Planet Earth is ominous. There are warnings that a million species of animal and plant life will be lost in the next 12 years unless we turn this trend around fast. A million species—it's almost an unimaginable loss!

But this natural holocaust should come as no surprise to anyone who has been following the news for the past 20 years. Chemical and industrial pollution are poisoning our lakes, streams, and the air we breathe. Oil spills are killing animals by the thousands and plant life too. Rain forests are being cut down for development at an alarming rate. The loss of wetlands to development has taken away the habitat of many animal and plant species. Acid rain, the greenhouse effect, nuclear wastes, all threaten to destroy us, and the list goes on.

Air pollution, too, threatens our planet's life. Ozone pollution can cause eye irritation and respiratory illness in terrestrial animals. Acid rain causes permanent damage to fish. Toxic concentrations of metals and ozone pollution are having severe effects on aquatic ecosystems. Fish and invertebrates are dying because of increased aluminum in the water and ozone pollution.

Pesticides, fertilizers, and herbicides are causing death among birds and other animals. Their usage has been increased in the last few years and they are finding their way into food and water supplies.

And of course any form of pollution or over-development that causes the destruction of habitat threatens the entire ecosystem—starting with the plants at the bottom of the food chain and going right to the top, to us.

## "I Just Wanted to See Something Die."

You'd think we'd learn, but the human species does not seem to get the message. As the environmental devastation continues, we help it along with a thriving "sport" called hunting. Endangered animals are poached for their horns or ivory. Others are hunted for trophies, their heads with horns or antlers proudly displayed on the hunter's walls. The horror of hunting reminds me of a particularly apt quote:

> *"Wild animals never kill for sport. Man is the only one to whom the torture and death of his fellow creatures is amusing in itself."*
>
> —James Anthony Froude

Tragically, our national parks and wildlife refuges are open to hunters whenever a population of animals is declared by wildlife managers to be too large. The multi-million dollar hunting and fishing industry takes full, lusty advantage of the situation, not just through legal hunting and fishing but also through poaching. Illegal killing of animals keeps our game wardens and other officials working overtime. As reported in *Defenders* magazine (May/June 1988, "Yellowstone's Poaching War," by Todd Wilkinson), the bloodthirstiness of the poachers is appalling.

Jackson Hole warden Doug Crawford told Todd Wilkinson, "It goes back to the days of Robin Hood and Sherwood Forest. People believe it is their God-given right to take the King's game." It is estimated that 99 percent of poaching cases do not involve hunting for food.

Game management specialists tell sordid tales of bears, swans, deer, and bald eagles being shot and just left to die. One warden says, "It's scary. I always ask the suspects what motivated them to fire upon animals. One guy told me, 'At that moment I just had to kill something.' Another said, 'I just wanted to see something die.'"

In Alaska, big game hunters operating under the authority of legal trapping permits have used airplanes to spot wolverines, wolves, and foxes. Once they sighted their quarry, they would land and shoot them. Fortunately, this practice was banned for shooting wolverines and foxes, but was allowed to continue in some areas for wolves.

To satisfy an inconceivable lust for killing, men have hunted some animals to extinction and others to severe endangerment, where the only surviving members of that species are in national parks and zoos.

While laws to protect wild animals are on the books, the vastness of our wild lands poses a tremendous law enforcement problem. The Greater Yellowstone area alone covers four million acres of wilderness. Poachers can easily escape the grasp of park officials. Few are arrested; even fewer are sentenced to prison terms.

All over the world, the poaching problem is fueled by an incomprehensible desire for exotic animal products. In America, poachers who sell exotic animal products are after trophy-class bighorn sheep, bear claws and gall bladders, bald eagle feathers, and live falcons. There are actually individuals who collect these "world-class trophies" and will pay thousands of dollars for them, as if they were buying works of art.

In Africa and Asia, the problem is even more severe. Illegal trade in rhino horns has reduced the population of black rhinos to only about 4,000. The demand for ivory has led poachers to undertake extraordinary measures, including the murder of wildlife officials, to get at their prey. As a result, the elephant population in Africa has declined 36 percent in the last six years. It is estimated that 89,000 elephant tusks entered the trade illegally in one year.

Is there hope that we might end poaching? Here in America, the answer is "yes"—if we as a nation are willing to make a sizable investment. It is estimated that it costs the Fish and Wildlife Service at least $200,000, plus the full-time use of an undercover officer for at least a year, to infiltrate just one poaching ring! In developing countries in Africa and Asia, such investment may not be possible. We can only hope that, with assistance from international organizations like the World Wildlife Fund and others, these nations will find a way to preserve their extraordinary natural wildlife legacies.

## Peril in and on the Seas

Marine animals, too, face the grave dangers of pollution and hunting. The great oceans provide no relief from the human-created problems that plague earth-bound creatures!

Pollution in many forms threatens to destroy our oceans and the creatures inhabiting them. Today, marine animals must contend with a new threat, courtesy of our throw-away society: plastic debris. Annually, many thousands of animals, including whales, porpoises, sea turtles, seals, sea birds, and fish, fall victim to discarded plastic products, which they sometimes eat, thinking, for example, that a piece of styrofoam might be a delectable morsel of fish. The animals also become accidentally entangled in old fishing gear, strapping bands, plastic six-pack holders, and other types of plastic trash. After becoming entangled, the animal may then drown, strangle, be unable to eat or swim, or die from a plastic-induced cut that becomes infected.

Chemical pollution from a multitude of sources is also choking off life in the ocean, bays, and rivers. The oil spill in Alaska is a particularly disastrous example. Current estimates now put the number of birds killed from this spill at 13,000. They died from being oiled directly or from eating food or water that had been oiled. Between 4,000 and 6,000 otters died. Deer, ducks, puffins, and other creatures have also suffered and died from this industrial accident. Even though thousands of people worked to save these animals, nothing could be done. There is no way to measure the damage this one spill caused to the environment.

Like their land-animal counterparts, marine creatures must also contend with man's hunting and harvesting efforts. Some animals, including several species of sea turtles and whales, have been pushed to the brink of extinction because of carelessness or greed on the part of commercial fishermen.

Though not yet threatened by extinction, dolphins may soon be on the endangered species list because of fishing abuses. Dolphins have been historically treated as friends by fishermen, who used them as indicators to locate schools of yellowfin tuna, which, for reasons still unknown, swim beneath the herds of dolphins. In the 1960s, the fishermen began using new technologies—giant hydraulic power blocks, big nylon nets, speedboats, helicopters, and a method known as purse seining. Using this method, a herd of dolphins is sighted and rounded up by speedy boats with loud, whining engines powerful enough to interfere with the dolphin's sensitive sonar communication system. Sometimes fishermen throw small explosives in the water too. The dolphins are boxed in by the mass of tuna below them. The purse seine net surrounds and tightens around them and they are smashed together.

It is estimated that about seven million dolphins

have been killed in tuna fishing in the last 25 years. This practice is used only in the eastern tropical Pacific Ocean from mid-California to mid-Chile. The tuna caught in this area supplies only about five percent of the world's tuna catch. The other 95 percent is caught without killing the dolphins.

The greed for whales has caused dramatic declines in the world's population of blue whales, the largest mammal ever to live on our planet. Now so few of these mighty animals remain that it may no longer be possible for them to reproduce effectively. Other once-common whale species are also severely threatened, including the humpback and right whales, species which once populated every coastline.

The international conservation community has asked whaling nations to stop all whaling activity. But even when the nations agree to do so, such treaties are difficult to enforce. For example, though Japan signed an agreement to phase out their whaling, there are still reports of whales being taken by the Japanese, who claim these animals are to be used for research.

## Is There Hope?

Where there is still life, there is hope. Where animals have already been lost to extinction, hope is gone forever. But we must continue to struggle to preserve what we have left, the beautiful flora and fauna of this once-pristine earth.

As a society, we need more acquisition, restoration, and protection of key habitats. We need to rally around legislation that will preserve our wild lands and keep the poachers away from innocent wild animals. We need to speak out for conservation at every possible opportunity.

For the animals now on the endangered species list, we can still hope. Zoos are attempting to breed many of these rare and endangered animals successfully. However, this can only be done in very small numbers, and certainly it is no substitute for the natural state of the earth, in which animals could live undisturbed in their natural habitats.

As the Defenders of Wildlife ask, "How in the world will tomorrow's children know the wonder of wildlife if there's no wildlife left in the world?" I hope you will join with me to make sure that your children and their children will be able to witness the great array of wild animals—and, indeed, to make sure that there will still be a healthy environment for animals *and* man for generations yet to come.

# CHAPTER 7

# A Haven and a Refuge: Peace Plantation

For the 18 years of my marriage to Briggsie, I knew what it meant to be truly in love. To me, the man was an angel—a loving husband, a gentle father, a tireless worker for the innocent animals who could not help themselves.

Once married, we moved to the Be Kind to Animals Rest Farm, living in part of the caretaker's house. I got used to kerosene heaters, oil lamps, and an oil cookstove once again. Now, too, I learned to carry water long distances, in buckets, uphill when our rusty old pump broke down, as it often did. People think of these things as hardships, and perhaps I would, too, if I had to do them again today, but at that time they did not seem so difficult, because we shared all the work.

My life was happy and busy. I drove Briggsie to work in Washington six days a week. Three times a week, I went to a bakery to buy two-day-old bread for our animals, and then on to an abattoir (a slaughterhouse) to get the cheapest available meats, beef lungs and livers. I hated going there, hearing the animals being driven to their slaughter, but I had no choice: Our animals had to eat.

Then I'd go back to the farm and help prepare the food for 200 dogs and 70 cats. Fortunately, we could feed the larger animals, horses and cattle, on the hay and grain the farm produced. Then, when the animals had all been fed for the day, I'd drive back to Washington and pick up my husband. Often, on the return trip, we'd stop to pick up an animal to take back to the farm with us.

After his workday was done, Briggsie spent long hours taking care of the animals and repairing kennels. In fact, this was the pattern for the rest of his life: Work all day at a demanding office job, then work at night and on the weekends in his efforts to help animals. In spite of this exhausting routine, I never heard my husband say "I'm tired." Though in later years he became a bit stooped from leaning over his desk for so many hours, his abundant love for life never abated.

## The Briggs Family Grows

When people ask me today how I keep going in spite of discouragements, I tell them I learned my optimism from Briggsie. I don't believe he knew how to get really discouraged—though he had some hard blows, especially when we lost the Be Kind to Animals Rest Farm.

With the arrival of our first child in March 1929,

we had been forced to move to more congenial living quarters in the city with running water and electricity, but we managed to keep the Farm, working there in our spare hours. Back in Washington, D.C., I managed to continue taking stale bread and cheap meat to the Farm, hiring a babysitter to watch our son Jimmy while I took these trips. Times were hard. Often we found ourselves having to beg or borrow money in order to feed the animals at the Farm. How I hated pleading for money! I had no choice, with so many mouths to feed, but I detested it nonetheless.

We tried many avenues to make some extra income, including opening a candy store. I learned to make candy and worked hard, long hours turning out all sorts of delectable items, but still we found it hard to come out ahead.

Though we continued the candy business, hoping that it might turn a real though modest profit someday, things only got worse for us financially. Of course, there was still much joy in our lives: Our son Bobby was born in April 1931, and we continued our work with the animals, though under increasingly difficult conditions. But in 1932, the economic disaster known as the Depression finally robbed us of our farm. For want of $6,500, we lost it. And though I was not too proud to beg on behalf of my animals, there was no way to raise this enormous sum of money in those bleak days.

We were heartbroken, but there was nothing we could do other than try our best to find homes for the animals then at the farm. With the help of Mrs. Kibbie of Bide-A-Wee, a humane organization in

New York which took in 150 of our least-likely-to-be-adopted dogs, we placed every animal in a good home.

And so it was that the doors closed on the Be Kind to Animals Rest Farm. Briggsie turned his attention to the needs of animals in laboratories and steel traps. As for me, I closed the candy store in 1933, choosing to find a job with a regular income. But first, with Briggsie's encouragement, I decided to return to high school and get my diploma, which I received in 1936. Fortunately, a kind, loving, and dependable woman named Ruby Brown had come into our lives; Ruby helped with our children while I attended classes. She was a great blessing to our growing family, especially when son, Jack, was born in 1934 and daughter, Virginia, in 1937.

I named my daughter Virginia after my friend Virginia Sargent, President of the Animal Protective Association, who ran an animal shelter. I helped Miss Sargent whenever I could in the kennels; she in turn allowed me to board animals in need at her facility until good homes could be found for them. Thanks to Miss Sargent, I was able to continue the animal rescue work Briggsie and I had been so devoted to at the farm. During these years I also worked with a lady named Alice Morgan Wright. We who loved animals formed a network all around the area, doing whatever we could to help animals. Both Miss Sargent and Miss Wright were instrumental in my work and to the National Humane Education Society as it exists today.

These were busy years, with my young family,

my animal rescue work, and, as of April 1941, a secretarial job with the U.S. Army. Since Briggsie was so much older than me, I realized that I needed to prepare myself to support my children. The last thing I wanted was to be unable to keep my family together if my husband died—the same thing that had happened to my mother, splitting our family apart. Since Briggsie's health was not good, I urged him to retire. But this hard-working family man would not hear of it.

On December 7, 1941, as the Pearl Harbor attack was announced over the radio, Briggsie and I were signing papers to buy a house in Riverdale, Maryland. We moved our family there, and from then on both of us worked six days a week, and, because of the war, often on Sundays, too.

Despite our long, hard hours and our concerns for our nation and its allies, our family was thriving during those war years. Jimmy, our oldest son, had excelled in school. He graduated from high school in 1945, at the age of 15, and was accepted early by the Georgetown University School of Foreign Service. That summer was a good one for our children, who loved living in Riverdale and had many friends.

Briggsie was working harder than ever to spare dogs from vivisection, pushing for the passage of the Dog Exemption Bill by Congress. On September 8, 1945, he traveled to Philadelphia to talk with colleagues there about the proposed legislation. I picked him up upon his return at Union Station, noticing how very tired he looked and how slowly he walked toward the car. He did not say much and I did not press him for details of his visit.

We had gone only a few blocks when he asked me to stop for a bit. I wanted to take him to the doctor, but he said no. I soon realized that he was going into a coma. I rushed him to a hospital, but the shot of adrenalin he was given did not revive him.

Jimmy and Jack were with me. I hugged my sons as I broke the news of their father's death. Then we went home to tell Bob and Virginia, or Ginger, as she is called. My children had never known death before. They had never even been to a funeral! The boys tried not to burden me with their sorrow, spending a lot of time together in their big bedroom. Ginger, though, was bewildered, and clung to me.

We decided it would be easier to leave our Riverdale house, with its many reminders of Briggsie, and to start anew. We sold it and moved to a house in Washington with more affordable payments. I realized that I must find an additional source of income. Fortunately, Virginia Sargent offered me work doing bookkeeping for her shelter. My two older sons graduated from school and went to work, Jimmy at the State Department and Bobby at a bank. As a family, we pulled together, and I am so grateful for that.

## Peace Plantation Is Born

All through these sad times, of course, we still carried on in our work for animals. In 1948, Alice Morgan Wright, who was—among other things—an heiress, an animal rights activist, an organizer of the United Nations Educational, Scientific, and Cultural

Organization (UNESCO), and a sculptress—approached me with an idea.

"Anna, we need to start a national organization," she said, "so we can do the most effective work possible for the animals."

Together, Miss Wright and I started the National Humane Education Society that year. Its guiding principles, reproduced at the back of this book, were authored by Miss Wright, a great lady whose contributions to the well-being of animals are legion.

At about this time, Miss Sargent, who had been running the shelter I worked with, told me she was going to have to close it down. Now I knew I would no longer have a place to house strays and rescued animals. This worried me greatly. I told Miss Wright about the situation, and she promised financial backing to start a shelter under the auspices of our Society.

My son, Jimmy, and I went out looking for a suitable place. After quite a search, we found a 145-acre place in Sterling, Virginia, with a large house and garage, two sheds and a chicken house. Its price was $50,000. Miss Wright came from Albany to look at it, and offered to donate half the purchase price. Jimmy and I decided to take her up on it, and we would meet the monthly payments of this first shelter of the National Humane Education Society.

We sold our house in Washington, receiving about $6,000 in equity, which we used to put up a frame building large enough to house about 50 dogs. My sons used their heads and their hands to do the enormous amount of work that built our first Peace Plantation, including piping water from a lake uphill to the kennels, erecting pens, and painting and concreting.

## A Lady Named Ruby:
### The Heart and Soul of Peace Plantation

As we prepared for the move to Sterling, I realized how badly we would need help in caring for the animals. I turned to my old friend, Ruby Brown, a Black woman who had helped me for years by babysitting for my children when they were little, when I was working or helping at the Be Kind to Animals Rest Farm. Ruby was a widow with six children, living at home in an inner-city area of Washington. Rats were frequent visitors in that neighborhood, and it was not the best environment in which to raise children.

I didn't know if Ruby would want to come to Sterling, Virginia to be the chief animal caretaker of Peace Plantation. And in those days, in Virginia, hiring a Black person for such a responsible post was nearly unheard-of. But Ruby's color never concerned me. I wanted the kindest, most loving, most competent person for the most important job at Peace Plantation. So I asked Ruby, "Would you like to come live in the country?"

"I sure would," she said. Her curiosity was piqued.

I told her what her duties would be if she accepted my offer to work and live at Peace Plantation: fixing enormous quantities of food for cats and dogs, cleaning their pens and litter boxes, going on emergency rescue missions—whatever it would take to give hundreds of needy animals the best possible care.

It wasn't a job for just anybody, I explained.

"How will I know how to take care of cats and dogs?" Ruby asked me.

"You'll learn," I told her, chuckling. "They'll teach you!"

God was good to me that day. Ruby said "yes," and moved with us to Peace Plantation on July 1, 1950, its first day of operation. Without Ruby, there is no way we could have handled the quickly growing reputation of Peace Plantation as a great place to take animals in trouble—a place where no healthy animal would ever be euthanized!

My boys converted an open shed into a small house for her, a place she referred to proudly as "my little white house." At first, I could offer her only a very paltry salary, in addition to her room and board. Later, I'm glad to report, the Society was able to pay Ruby more appropriately—but of course no amount of money could ever pay for the kind of love and caring she gave to thousands of animals in her years at Peace Plantation.

Ruby stayed with us in Sterling, then moved again when we relocated Peace Plantation to Leesburg, Virginia, in 1965. For 34 years, Ruby was the heart and soul of Peace Plantation, my right arm and half of my left. Knowing that Ruby was in charge, I could leave our place to go rescue animals or to raise the money we so desperately needed to keep our operation going. Ruby took to her duties as if she had been doing them all her life, greeting all guests and giving tours to school and civic groups. No animal rescue effort was too strenuous for her. And she loved the animals so much that she would go out of her way to prepare treats for them—stopping on the roadside to pick watercress to add to their meals, making corn on the cob with margarine for the cats, fixing up any little delicacy that might add pleasure to their lives. (Yes, cats like watercress, corn on the cob—and potatoes!)

"I try not to favor any cat or dog in our charge," she would say, "and I strive to pass my love to all of them in my care. No task is too menial when it comes to tending the cats and dogs."

Removing leftover food and cleaning litter boxes never seemed to bother Ruby. Nor did washing the carpets and rugs from the animals' pens—by hand, on a washboard, because Peace Plantation didn't have a washer or a dryer in those days. We all shared in this heavy work. Ruby never complained of it. She felt it was a privilege to take care of the animals.

Ruby's love and dedication showed—in the animals' sparkling-clean cages, in their odor-free quarters, in their healthy coats and eyes, and in their happy demeanor. People from all over the region and even across the country got to know Ruby well when they brought animals to us or adopted them from us.

"Ruby *was* Peace Plantation," people told me when she died.

That was a terrible day, the day Ruby died.

It was September 8, 1984. I was away from home, in New York City, in the tunnels beneath Grand Central Station. My work there had started in 1972. Two railroad employees had been feeding the wild cats who lived in the station's underground area, but now they were about to retire. They were worried about what would happen to the animals. I went back several times in that first year or so, bringing back many cats to Peace Plantation. Others who helped with the rescue promised to keep an eye out to make sure no more cats remained. They promised to call me if they saw others who needed our help.

I didn't hear from them until 1984, when they asked me to come and rescue many more cats now living there. I put my humane traps out as always, but got only one cat and one kitten. It turned out that some well-meaning ladies, fearing I would nab the cats and have them put to sleep, had fed them already that morning!

Greatly discouraged, I called home to check on matters at Peace Plantation, as I always did when I was travelling. To my horror, I learned that Ruby had been taken ill and sent by ambulance to the hospital.

I got back to Leesburg as fast as I could, but by the time I arrived, Ruby had died of a heart attack. She was 76 years old, one year older than me, and she had been my friend since we met on my 18th birthday. I felt my whole world had come to an end. Of course, the world did not end. No matter how heartbroken we might be, life has a way of going on in spite of our feelings. And we had new challenges to meet.

The area around Peace Plantation was starting to become very fashionable in the early 1980s, as the Washington, D.C. metropolitan area continued to expand into the countryside. My daughter, Virginia, and I had a discussion in 1982 about what we would do if the farms surrounding the Plantation were sold off, subdivided, and developed. Surely people buying fancy new homes would not want to be near a thriving animal shelter like ours. Anticipating changes in the area zoning, we started looking for a new place.

At first we asked one of our neighbors if they would sell us 100 acres. This, we figured, would be adequate "insulation" between us and any encroaching suburban community. Certainly, said the neighbor, for $400,000! We laughed. Such a price tag was out of the question! We had been operating on a shoestring for years. For years, I had worked full-time at my Government job, running the Society and Peace Plantation in the evenings and on weekends. Of course I would have preferred to devote all my time to Peace Plantation, but financial reality would not allow it—just as financial reality made $400,000 an impossibility.

Because property was so expensive in our area, we looked in neighboring states—West Virginia and Pennsylvania. But nothing turned up there, so we kept looking, going into rural New York. At last, we found a 138-acre farm near Walton, a small town in upstate New York. The farm had a small kennel and a very nice stable we could use as temporary quarters for the animals.

In 1983, the Society's Board of Directors approved the purchase of the Walton farm, and endorsed our decision to create the new Peace Plantation there. In May, my daughter's husband, Earl Dungan, went to Walton to get the operation started. So by the time of Ruby's death in September 1984, things were well under way at Walton. It seemed to me that Earl had worked miracles with our new facility, which we moved into late in 1984, taking many trips in our station wagon or pickup truck to transport our animals from Leesburg to Walton.

I only wished that Ruby had been able to share our joy as we dedicated our new facility to the ongoing work of the National Humane Education Society. At first, it didn't feel like Peace Plantation, because Ruby was not there to make it so. But today, in my mind's eye, I can imagine this great lady playing Pied Piper to the hundreds of cats in our much-improved facility in Walton, sharing with them her unbounded love and devotion. And somehow, I think Ruby's spirit is still with us, still blessing our work as only she could do.

Heaven knows we need her still, as the requests to help needy, hurt, frightened animals continue to pour in to our offices, and as we strive to meet their needs, doing our best to be one candle in the darkness of a cold, cruel world.

# CHAPTER 8

# Some Lives Are Cheap: The Tragedy of Animal Overpopulation

*"Recollect that the Almighty, who gave the dog to be the companion of our pleasures and our toils, hath invested him with a nature noble and incapable of deceit."*

—Sir Walter Scott

One day some years ago, I was told of a mother dog and her puppies, homeless, camped out in a park in Washington, D.C. Clearly, the pregnant dog had been abandoned by a callous owner to bear her pups on her own.

When I was told about this dog, I knew I had to hurry to save her, because the animal warden in Washington at that time, a Mr. King, would undoubtedly soon be on the scene.

If Mr. King got her first, she and her puppies would go to the pound. Then, within a few days, they would all almost certainly meet their death.

I went as quickly as I could to the park, where I found the mother and her pups under a big sycamore tree. As I neared her, the mother snarled and growled at me, protecting her puppies. I put out my humane trap and prepared to wait, quietly talking to the dog all the while.

Sure enough, Mr. King soon made his entrance. Rather than wait patiently for the animal to make her way into the trap, Mr. King went after her. Naturally, she took off running; any mother dog would have done that, to divert attention away from her pups. I hurriedly put the puppies in the dog trap as bait, feeling certain the mother would run into the trap to protect them. Fortunately for me, she did.

"Got her now!" exclaimed Mr. King triumphantly.

"I beg your pardon," I said pleasantly, "but that's *my* trap—and that's *my* dog!"

Mr. King sighed. "I guess you've got me there," he said. I took the mother and her pups to Peace Plantation. After three days of loving care and feeding, the mother dog understood that we only wanted to help her and her little ones. Eventually, she was spayed, and she and her pups were given away to excellent adoptive homes.

My friendly rivalry with Mr. King continued for years. For, though I knew this good man had the best of intentions, I also knew that any homeless animal that fell into his hands would almost certainly be euthanized in his shelter.

This is still true today. In fact, the situation is only getting worse. For lack of homes, 10 million healthy dogs and cats are destroyed by animal shelters and pounds each year. Countless millions of others, abandoned by unfeeling owners, roam streets and alleyways until they are killed or die of disease, starvation, or extremes of temperature.

The root of all this suffering and wasted life? Animal overpopulation. The principal reason for this tragic destruction of animals is society's permissiveness toward the breeding of its pets and it unwillingness to accept long-term responsibility for pets' lives. No animal shelter likes the job of killing the vast numbers of unwanted animals.

Animal overpopulation did not become a problem until well into the 20th century. Before then, people had fewer pets. Pets were not overbred. And those who died were replaced by adopting others.

As house pets became popular, procreation quickly outstripped demand. The situation was made worse by the unwillingness of owners to care for their pets over their full lifetimes, or to find suitable homes for them when they could no longer keep them.

The huge numbers of abandoned and unwanted cats and dogs have inundated America's animal shelters. Although they have done their best to encourage adoptions, shelters have been able to place fewer than three out of ten shelter animals in suitable homes since the 1960s. The only solution for the remaining 70 percent? Euthanasia. After a few days in the shelter, animals must be destroyed so that others who come after them can be handled as humanely as possible.

If ever there was a treadmill to disaster for dogs and cats, surely it is our shelter system. Of course, the National Humane Education Society has created an exception to this terrible rule. At Peace Plantation, an animal will not be euthanized unless it is terribly ill, in pain, and without any hope of recovery.

Ours is a standard most shelters cannot meet. The shelters have been criticized for using euthanasia. But the fault really lies with the public—for overbreeding, for not having pets spayed or neutered, and for not accepting responsibility for the pet's lifelong care.

Humane officials have had to accept euthanasia as a short-term solution to the overpopulation of pets brought to the shelters. At the same time, they are actively seeking a much better long-term solution.

Pound seizure is another sad fate that awaits many of the abandoned and unwanted animals brought to shelters. This terrible practice involves selling or releasing dogs and cats to laboratories for biomedical experiments. Animal rights activists, including my late husband, have fought pound seizure for almost 50 years.

The first state law mandating the practice of pound seizure was passed in Minnesota in 1948. Only twelve states have laws forbidding this practice: Massachusetts, Maine, New Hampshire, Vermont, Rhode Island, Connecticut, Maryland, Delaware, Hawaii, New York, New Jersey, and Pennsylvania. Although many of the remaining states do not require pound seizure, they allow it.

As I mentioned in this book's chapter on vivisection, after World War II, biomedical research with live animals increased tremendously. More money was made available for this research. More people were attending universities and going into research. Today's highly profitable industries that breed animals for laboratory use did not yet exist.

At the same time, the population began shifting to urban areas. Pets came to the cities with their owners. The shelters had been built when most animals didn't stray far from the farm. Now, they were overburdened with this increase of animals in the city. Pound seizure proponents rationalized that animals in the shelter were going to die anyway. Why not use them for research? That would be taking only one animal's life, not two, and it would save money.

Humane organizations argue that animals chosen for the laboratory are the ones most likely to be adopted—young, one to three years of age, healthy, friendly, and of medium size. Those who are rejected are the animals least likely to find adoptive homes.

The Society and other animal rights groups are trying to educate owners to be responsible and fight pet overpopulation. We want to make people aware that pets are not disposable items—to be discarded when one is tired of them or they're too much trouble. By allowing pound seizure, we're placing a cheap price on animal life—allowing shelters to serve as discount warehouse suppliers for biomedical research laboratories.

Animals endure incalculable pain and suffering, and many lose their lives, all because their owners won't accept lifelong responsibility for pets—and because pet owners refuse to have their pets spayed or neutered.

People cite two popular myths to explain why they are unwilling to take their pets to veterinarians for neutering. The first myth is that it is inhumane to sterilize animals and deprive them of their sex lives. The second is that animals who are sterilized get fat and lazy and lose interest in playing and responding to loving care.

Neither of these assumptions is correct.

Spaying (removing the uterus, tubes, and ovaries of a female animal) and neutering (a term used for the altering of both sexes, including the removal of testicles in the male) are routine operations. They are done under general anesthesia. The operation does not significantly change the personality of the pet. For females, it actually lessens their irritability at certain times of the year and it reduces breast cancer in later life. Unaltered males often get kidney problems and sometimes prostate cancer.

Nor does neutering make the pets fat, lazy, or aloof. This idea arose because animals are neutered around the time they emerge from puppyhood and kittenhood, a time in life when they will put on weight if they are overfed and under-exercised. In that respect, they are just like their owners!

There is no tragedy in preventing a pet from reproducing. The sex life of a pet is governed by glandular discharges of hormones and is free of the social forces that surround human sexuality. If they are sterilized before they mate, the pets don't know about sex and don't miss it.

Sometimes owners don't have the pets neutered because of cost. The operation for cats costs less than that for dogs and it costs less for males than for females. The cost for proper care of a pet is something that should be considered before deciding to become a pet owner. For those who truly can't afford the expense of the operation, there are agencies that offer financial assistance. For example, the Friends of Animals headquartered in Neptune, New Jersey, recently helped to finance 70,000 dog and cat spaying and neutering operations through a network of some 800 participating veterinarians in 46 states.

An interesting note is that a recent study done by CEN/SHARE, the University of Minnesota's Center to Study Human-Animal Relations, found that female dogs are much more likely to be spayed than male dogs to be neutered. "These results may reflect human societal norms, which assign contraceptive decisions and fertility control to the female," explained Dr. M. Geraldine Gage, a professor in Family Social Science who co-authored the study with Dr. Robert K. Anderson, associate director of CEN/SHARE.

As a pet owner, you must realize and accept the responsibility that you have for this animal. Of the 3,500 shelters in the United States, only about a dozen rule out euthanasia as a matter of policy.

That's how few shelters today share the policy of our Peace Plantation. In peaceful, home-like surroundings, healthy animals are able to live out their lives naturally at Peace Plantation unless they are placed for adoption in other good homes.

The Society is opposed to euthanasia as a means of population control for any animal. None of the dogs and cats at Peace Plantation is ever put to sleep simply to make room for another. This upbeat philosophy of setting a high value on animal life has a down side, however: It places a limit on the number of strays the shelters can accept. At its current operating capacity, for example, Peace Plantation can care for some 600 cats and 50 dogs, the shelter's present population. (Many extra dogs are boarded at public kennels.)

In recent years, shelters have spent much of their resources educating the public, particularly young people, about the lifetime commitment pet owners should be willing to make, and about the need to control the pet population. Our Society has spread this humane message through its publications and our mass mailings. Still, much more needs to be done.

The problem of overpopulation must be conquered and this treadmill to destruction must be stopped. Whatever the reason—getting tired of the pet, lack of proper training when the animal has bad habits such as chewing, soiling the house, etc., deciding the care of the pet is too expensive, not having the pet altered—when you decide to take a pet to the pound, you can be almost certain that the pet will have to be put to sleep or, worse still, that it will become a victim of pound seizure. Think before you become a pet owner. Become a pet owner for life, not just for the holidays!

In addition to education, other measures advocated by humane organizations like the National Humane Education Society include the following:

• Local governments should provide financial assistance for spaying and neutering programs where needed. Monies allocated for this purpose will eventually come back to the community many times over, as fewer resources are required to care for a reduced stray population. For example, the Humane Society of Charlotte, North Carolina, experienced a 30 percent reduction in stray, owner-relinquished, and abandoned cats and dogs, following a spay/neuter program that sterilized 10,000 animals in a four-year period.

• Animals adopted from shelters should be sterilized to prevent further breeding. This is done as a matter of course at Peace Plantation. No pet is permitted to be adopted unless it has first been neutered. Adopted pets should not be adding their own litters to the unwanted population.

• Local governments should require all cats and dogs to be licensed and tagged. Tags help officials locate owners of lost pets which otherwise might end up in shelters. Computerization has added to the efficiency in locating pets with tags.

• Adoption programs should be strengthened so more animals from shelters can be given homes. Of course, this alone won't empty shelters, but it will at least cut down on the number of animals that have to be destroyed for lack of room.

• The public should be encouraged to donate time and money to help local shelters and organizations expand their educational programs. Local governments are burdened with so many budget requests and problems that there is a limited amount they can do. This underscores the importance of the voluntary, not-for-profit organizations such as the National Humane Education Society. These organizations can add a great deal of support to local government animal control programs. An example of organizations working together with government is a group of 19 voluntary organizations in Ohio who pooled their educational resources to meet a state goal of reducing by half the number of homeless, unwanted, and abandoned dogs and cats.

The nation needs more cooperation between the public and private sectors. We need more men and women who will join in the crusade to put an end to this national disgrace—the needless destruction of millions of healthy, loving animals every year.

The challenge to work to this end was expressed very well by Carol Moulton of the American Humane Association, writing in *Animals Agenda*:

> There are those who feel that dog and cat over-population—like the poor—will always be with us. They accept the need for euthanasia as a fact of life, not as a temporary necessity. They do not believe it will ever be possible to reduce the number of unwanted animals to the point where mass killing is not a daily task at most animal shelters. Though it is likely that there always will be some human-caused animal suffering, dog and cat overpopulation is a finite problem. It had a beginning, it had identifiable causes, and now it is starting to have identifiable solutions.

The challenge is to recognize the solutions, refine and improve them, and put them to work all over the country.

> —Carol Moulton, "Animal Overpopulation: A Treadmill to Disaster," *Animals Agenda*, May 1988.

## The Puppy Mill Scandal

Most people are attracted to puppies and kittens. "How Much Is That Doggie in the Window?" has become one of the classic songs at Christmas time. Walking by a pet shop and seeing cute, playful little puppies or kittens makes it hard to resist becoming a pet owner. Every year, as many as 500,000 puppies are sold in pet stores.

There is no doubt that puppies and kittens are appealing. It takes a strong will to put aside that appeal for a moment, and to think through the decision to acquire a pet, weighing the responsibilities that come with that pet carefully.

If you decide to purchase or adopt a pet, ask yourself questions like these: If the pet is for a child, is the child old enough to care for a puppy? Will my home offer long-term care for this animal? Is there a chance my child or I will tire of the pet? Will it be abandoned with the tree and tinsel and end up in the pound to be "put to sleep" because no one wants it any longer?

It is heart-breaking to think what will happen to the puppy or kitten if no one cares. It is even more sobering to think of what happens in many commercial kennels and pet stores because the kennel and store owners look at the pets only from the viewpoint of a profit.

All too often, "puppy mills" have no feeling for the well being of the precious lives they helped to create. Only outright, callous contempt for life can explain the grotesque conditions into which many of them breed and keep these helpless little animals.

A few years ago, Robert Baker, an inspector of the Humane Society of the United States, conducted a survey of puppy mills in the U.S. More than half of them failed miserably to meet approved standards for housing, feeding, and sanitation.

The violations he found would make you sick. The owners had piled fecal material in two-foot-high piles in the dog runs. Puppies' feet were painfully stuck in the wire-mesh floors of their cages. And the puppies were fed the dead carcasses of other dogs!

Despite the public outcry and reforms that Mr. Baker's report precipitated, conditions in many puppy mills remain atrocious. In 1987, Mr. Baker made a spot inspection of 25 puppy mills at random and found them to be as bad, and in many cases worse, than what he had found in 1981.

Often puppy mill kennels consist of small wood and wire-mesh cages or empty crates outdoors. In many situations, female dogs are bred continuously without any rest between heat cycles. When the continuous breeding takes its toll on females, they are killed. It is common to find the mothers and their litters suffering from malnutrition, exposure, and lack of proper veterinary care.

The bad conditions don't end here. Inhumane treatment is often encountered in the shipping of the animals to pet stores and in the care the animals receive once they are on the retail market.

Because of the inhumane conditions under which animals are bred and shipped, Congress passed the Animal Welfare Act in 1966. The Animal Welfare Act is regulated by the Animal and Plant Health Inspection Service (APHIS) of the U.S. Department of Agriculture (USDA).

The law requires breeders to be licensed and authorizes APHIS to conduct inspections regularly and to follow up on complaints of inhumane conditions. Violators are given deadlines to correct their bad practices. A reinspection is made within 30 days to see if the recommendations have been carried out. If not, legal action is brought. Fines and penalties, including loss of license, may be applied.

While the law and inspections have helped conditions somewhat, there are still violations. Many humane groups challenge the USDA estimate of the number of substandard breeding kennels and think the inspectors may sometimes overlook bad practices. Due to Government budget restrictions, there are not enough inspectors to do the job properly. The USDA admits that it needs the help of the states and of the public at large to help eliminate the needless suffering that many animals now endure.

Humane groups and pet industry associations can help by educating and motivating breeders to follow proper operating procedures as well. But even if this humane protection network were working flaw-lessly, one big hole exists: Pet stores are not under the jurisdiction of APHIS regulation and inspection. Sub-ject only to local laws, rarely inspected, pet shops can and do get away with murder!

Horror stories have been told of owners buying pets who are sick. Often, the price will be reduced to get rid of a sick animal, or one the pet store has had for a long time. There are laws in some jurisdictions now that force the pet owner to refund the purchaser's money if the animal is sick. Officials hope this policy will encourage pet store owners to provide better care.

If they won't do it out of a sense of humane ethics, we can only try to force them to be kind by threatening their profits!

Transportation is another area where animals encounter abuse. Shipping from the pet breeders to the pet stores may be hundreds of miles. The animals are shipped in pickup trucks, tractor trailers, and planes, often without adequate food, water, ventila-tion, or shelter.

It is the position of the National Humane Educa-tion Society that the breeding, transportation, and sale of pets be done only under humane conditions to prevent needless suffering. This means requiring pet wholesalers, shipping companies, and pet shop retail-ers to maintain standards that will guarantee the well-being of the animals in their care.

The Society agrees with those who hold that inhu-mane conditions in the pet industry continue to be widespread and scandalous. We believe that education will help to redress those wrongs, but we are convinced that strict enforcement of Federal and local regulations is also essential. We think that more inspections are called for, particularly in the transportation and retail sale of pets. The pet industry has already proven that it cannot be trusted to regulate itself!

The Society believes that humane individuals and groups have a major role to play in preventing animal abuse:

1. We can report to the authorities operators found to be abusive of the pets in their care.

2. We can help establish and promulgate humane standards for the pet industry.

3. We can encourage people who want pets to adopt them from shelters, rather than buying them from pet stores or breeding kennels. We believe that it is unwise to breed many more hundreds of thousands of pets each year while the nation's shelters are over-crowded with unwanted and unclaimed pets destined for euthanasia or pound seizure.

"Buy me that doggie in the window!"

If you're sure it will get the care it deserves, say "Yes." Or better still, why not say "Yes" to the one in the window of Peace Plantation or other animal shelters? I can certainly guarantee you that you'll get just as much love and pleasure from one of our "orphans" as you would from a pet-shop animal!

They've got a lot of love to give, those 10 million animals that are being put to death each year. It breaks my heart to think about the tragic waste of their precious little lives!

# CHAPTER 9

# Glamour at Any Price: The Tragedy of the Fur Trade

*"For all wistful creatures in captivity . . . we ask a heart of compassion and gentle hands and kindly words."*

—Albert Schweitzer
"Prayer for Animals"

When I see someone wearing a fur coat, one image comes to mind, and it has nothing to do with fashion or glamour.

The image is of a fox with its tongue frozen to the metal of a steel trap, desperately struggling to free himself . . . desperately trying to hold onto life.

You see, the trappers put a grease on their traps that contains a scent designed to attract animals. So, naturally, the unsuspecting animal goes to lick the tasty-smelling grease. In winter, his tongue freezes to the cold metal.

In the trapper's mind, this is a perfect situation. The animal is trapped until he gets a chance to come back and check the trap—who knows, maybe several weeks from now. And best of all, the precious fur is unharmed!

There's nothing lovely about the fur trade. I agree whole-heartedly with the anti-fur campaign slogan, "It's a shame to wear fur!" Each year some 17 million wild animals are killed by trapping so their furs can be made into high-fashion garments. Another five million are raised and killed in abominable conditions on fur ranches. That's 22 million animals—foxes, wolves, coyotes, raccoons, bobcats, beavers, muskrats, otters, opossums, minks, among others—killed in the name of fashion!

Ninety percent of the animals trapped are caught in steel-jaw leghold traps. The teeth have been removed from the modern leghold trap, but it remains an effective, deadly, and inexpensive way of capturing and holding animals.

In some commercial trapping, a mechanical snare is used to catch, hold, and kill an animal for its pelt. This practice is the last vestige of the mass killing for profit with guns and traps that went on in this country in the 17th, 18th, and 19th centuries. Over the years, trapping has resulted in the decimation of enormous numbers of our nation's animal population. It continues today because of the value placed on furs as "fashion statements" for the rich and would-be rich.

Trapping has changed over the centuries, but its

legacy of shame and torture is still with us today. The American Indians trapped with primitive snares and covered pits dug in the ground, camouflaged to catch animals for food and hides. After Europeans arrived on the American continent, white trappers roamed the North American wilderness in search of animals for pelts to satisfy the Old World's insatiable demand for furs.

The Louisiana Purchase and exploration by Lewis and Clark opened much of the Northwest and high plains to colonization and trapping. In fact, the demand for furs was so lucrative that trappers led the way westward.

With the expansion of the fur trade came the development of new, more efficient traps and trapping techniques. One such invention was the infamous toothed-jawed leghold trap, invented by Seward Newhouse in 1823.

The leghold trap is a spring-powered snare with two metal jaws that snap shut on an animal's leg when it steps on a weight-sensitive trigger. Today, the leghold trap is made of steel, and the jaws no longer have teeth, but the more powerful spring snaps the jaws shut on the animal's body part with the force of a car door slamming on your hand!

The steel-jaw leghold trap, along with the gun, played a major role in the decline of wildlife in the 19th century. By the millions, beavers, bobcats, lynx, mink, skunks, raccoons, fishers, martens, wolverines, wolves, and bears were increasingly thinned by the deadly jaws that lay in wait for them throughout the once-benign wilderness.

By the end of the 19th century, leaders in business and Government, including Theodore Roosevelt, were outraged by the abusive practices and unsportsmanlike behavior of market hunters and trappers. They organized conservation clubs and began to lobby actively, supporting Government regulations to curb the orgy of unrestricted hunting and trapping. Market hunting was outlawed.

Currently, state departments of fish and wildlife carry out these regulations within their borders, limiting harvests to certain seasons and setting quotas on the kinds and number of animals that can be taken.

The cause of wild animal conservation was helped considerably in the early 1900s, when the demand for pelts declined in Europe and elsewhere. Many trappers went into other work when the demand for pelts lessened and the prices went down.

This hiatus didn't last long, though. After World War II, consumers began buying furs again. The rich prized them for fashion and status and a new middle-class market developed for cut-rate fur coats.

The snap of snares being sprung and the cries of animals in pain began to echo more and more in the wilderness. The most widely used trap continued to be the steel-jaw leghold. But there were—and are—others.

There is the Conibear trap, designed to ensnare the animal and kill it instantly by releasing a spring-loaded device that strikes the spinal column at the base of the skull with a crushing blow. Fortunately, this one isn't used often because it is unwieldy.

Other devices include a box-type trap that catches and holds the prey alive. It is also cumbersome and not widely used. Deadfall snares catch animals in concealed pits dug into the ground from which they cannot escape. This method is too labor-intensive to be popular among trappers.

Some people defend trapping as necessary to control the wild animal population, and thus to ensure the continued existence or health of the species and to preserve habitats that would be destroyed by overpopulation. Actually, wild animal populations are regulated by available food supplies and habitat naturally. Mother Nature does a pretty good job of that herself!

The fur industry and trappers aren't motivated by the desire to preserve or manage wildlife. They're motivated by the proceeds of a multi-million dollar industry.

Let's take a look at the trapper's version of "preservation of species and wildlife management."

The infamous steel-jaw leghold trap clamps down on the paw or limb of an animal with the force of a car door crushing a human hand and being left on it indefinitely—until someone comes to open it or the animal dies. Animals caught in these traps often bite off their own limbs trying to escape. This trap is considered so tortuous that it has been banned in over 65 countries. However, only four states in the United States have banned this horrible device.

The Conibear trap has the potential for causing prolonged agony by slowly strangling its victims over a period of several hours or several days.

Laws regarding the placement and handling of traps and how often they must be checked vary widely from state to state. Some states have no checking requirements. Trapped animals left for long periods of time very often suffer and die from dehydration, freezing, starvation, or exhaustion, or are eaten by predators. Even worse, some animals have been found alive after having been left in the traps for up to two weeks.

Trapped animals may be killed in any manner the trapper chooses, so long as it doesn't damage the pelt. No laws or requirements exist to determine how they are to be killed.

Popular methods used to kill the trapped animals include beating it to death with a blunt instrument; slamming its head against a tree or rock; stomping on its chest thus slowly suffocating the animal or crushing its heart; or drowning those trapped near water.

As the Friends of Animals' hard-hitting anti-fur message says, "Get a feel for fur. Slam your fingers in a car door."

The traps don't always capture the animals the trappers want to catch for pelts. An estimated five million "trash animals," such as domestic animals, wandering pets, endangered species, and unwanted wild animals accidentally wander into the traps and suffer agonizing deaths each year.

What can be done? People must refuse to buy furs, so that there will be no demand for them. Without the demand, it won't pay to trap these innocent victims.

Some people claim that fur farms offer a humane alternative to trapping in the wild as a source for pelts to be made into fur garments. But believe me, there is no humane way to make a fur coat!

More than five million wild animals, including minks, foxes, and chinchillas are raised and killed on American fur ranches each year. No laws or Government regulations now exist to oversee the living conditions of the animals or how they may be killed. The only standards that exist are unenforceable, voluntary guidelines created by the fur industry to try to pacify animal protectionists. Talk about the fox guarding the hen house!

These animals, whose natural habitats are in the wild where they may roam for miles, are kept in tiny, wire-mesh cages in which they barely have enough room to turn around. Many are almost insane with claustrophobia. They suffer from the heat during the hot times of the year. In 1987, 450,000 animals died due to heat stress, according to U.S. mink farmers. And this is the figure they *admit* to!

Animals raised on the fur ranches are killed in the most economical and convenient manner possible without damaging the pelt. Small animals, such as minks and chinchillas, are often killed by breaking their necks manually or mechanically.

Gassing the animals with carbon monoxide or carbon dioxide is another method used. This is done as cheaply as possible. The rancher channels exhaust fumes from a running motor vehicle into the animals' enclosures. The hot, unfiltered gas burns their eyes and lungs.

Poisons, including strychnine and cyanide, are used. Even paralytic drugs are occasionally administered.

The preferred method of execution for larger

animals such as foxes is electrocution. This is done by clamping an electrical cable in the fox's mouth while inserting another one into the animals's rectum. Animals experience extreme pain during electrocution and scream horribly.

Other methods used to kill animals raised on a fur ranch are drowning, tying an animal upside down and hitting it on the head, or putting chloroform on an animal's nose and imprisoning him in a can.

To meet the demand for cheaper furs, countries with lower wages are getting into the fur business. Korea, for example, has become one of the leading fur-manufacturing countries worldwide. Conditions there are even worse. Many die of heat stroke in the hot, humid summers. Often, cages are dirty with animals living in their own excrement. Killing methods are similar. In Korea, dogs are raised to be eaten as meat and to be stripped of their fur pelts, which are sold under the names of other animals. The publication *PETA News* estimates that more than one million dog furs are exported by North Korea every year!

The anti-fur message is being heard. Harvests are down, and business is slowing in chic fur salons across the nation. Citizens from all over the country are beginning to voice their concerns about fur. Letters opposing the sale of fur garments are being written to newspapers. People are complaining to department stores that sell furs; distributing educational materials about how fur-bearing animals are trapped, raised, and killed; and participating in anti-fur rallies.

Celebrities are joining the cause. *USA Today* has declared that "fur coats are out, cloth coats are in."

Some of the famous fashion designers have announced they will no longer design clothing made of fur. One of the committees of the World Council of Churches is working for an animal-protection platform which includes opposing wearing fur. Billboards placed prominently in our cities declare that "fur is out."

The National Humane Education Society and other humane organizations have been successful in raising the consciousness of many people. But I am eager to see even more progress immediately. It's so simple: If people refuse to buy fur garments, trapping will be halted and fur farms will have to go out of business.

What will be lost when the fur trade ends? Only the hideous pain and unnecessary deaths of millions of animals! It isn't as though fur coats and hats are necessary to guard against the cold. These days, clothing made of synthetic materials is just as warm as fur. It's also lighter, easier to clean, and much less expensive to replace.

The National Humane Education Society believes that there is no scientifically valid or ethical justification for commercial trapping. The Society has come to that conclusion for the following reasons:

1. Commercial trapping causes much needless suffering of fur creatures and many other wild and domestic animals caught in traps.

2. Most of the trapping is done with steel-jaw leghold traps, which we believe are inhumane.

3. Commercial trapping is motivated more by the desire for profit than by any imperative of wildlife management, and we believe that to be ethically

wrong.

4. Trapping is not scientifically valid as a wildlife management tool.

5. Nature does a better job of controlling populations of wildlife than does trapping.

6. Trapping fur creatures for pelts to be made into garments cannot be justified ethically. Outerwear made from man-made materials is just as protective and far less costly than furs.

7. Wearing fur garments to show off one's wealth is ethically wrong, because the pelts were obtained at the cost of much suffering to innocent animals.

Commercial trapping is a vestige of the days of unrestricted market hunting and trapping. Civilization demands better of modern society. Commercial trapping persists as a relic of a more brutish time, when living things were subject to mass slaughter, suffering, and even extinction to satisfy man's appetite for exotic foods, fancy furs, and superfluous frills.

It is time to outlaw commercial trapping. Only then can the needless suffering of animals caught in the steel jaws of leghold and other traps, or incarcerated in the unspeakable conditions of the "fur farms," be prevented.

As The Humane Society of the United States proclaims in its anti-fur campaign, "Fur is out, compassion is in." Together, we can save the lives of innocent animals, and make fur farming and trapping relics of the past.

# CHAPTER 10

# A Home for the Homeless: Peace Plantation Today

In my years of working with animals, I've gotten to know some wonderful people—people like Ruby Brown, like Alice Morgan Wright, like Virginia Sargent. And I've depended on these individuals to help get our enormous job done, just as others depend on us to help them care for their animals when they are no longer able.

So often we receive calls from elderly or ill people who find themselves unable to keep their beloved pets any longer. Heartbroken at the idea that they must give up their faithful companions, they must also try to protect them from euthanasia, the animals' certain fate should they go to the local pound.

I'll never forget one of these individuals—an elderly man called John. I heard about John through a lady who was a friend of mine. She had seen him in the check-out line of a grocery store in Washington, and noticed that he was buying nothing but cat food.

"You must have a lot of cats," she remarked to him.

"No, only two," he told her. "I can't afford any more."

My friend offered to help John by giving him some money. She was worried because he wasn't buying any food for himself, and she knew that often impoverished pet owners will go hungry rather than deprive their animals of food.

But John refused her offer, confiding that his immediate worry was not cash, but a place to live.

"I'm living in a rooming-house, and the landlady tells me I have to leave my quarters by the first of the month. I can't find a new place where I can take my cats and I just don't know what to do," he said.

My friend called me, arranging for me to come and get John's cats. He called these precious companions Itty and Bitty. The thought of parting from them was breaking his heart. When I met him, he started to cry.

"If I could only have gotten some work, maybe I could have found a home for them," he said. John was at least 80 years old at the time, and none too well, but I thought perhaps there was a chance he could find some gainful employment.

"Well, what do you do?" I asked him.

"I'm an auto mechanic. But I'd do anything. Even if I could find work as a gardener! Do you know anybody who needs a gardener?"

I wanted to laugh. I myself barely knew the difference between a rose and a dandelion, and Peace

Plantation was in dire need of somebody to keep the grounds in order. "I do!" I said, and I offered John the job in exchange for room and board for him and his cats.

He was thrilled. John and Itty and Bitty came to our place in April. By June, the gardens and lawns were beautiful. I thought I had a gold mine in John! Sadly, he died the following October. But he never had to be separated from his beloved animal friends, and, at the very end of his life, he knew the satisfaction of being useful, of being wanted, and of being cared for, even if it was only for a very short time.

John was like many of the animals we take in at Peace Plantation—not in the best of health, no longer in the prime of life, overlooked by an uncaring world. For me, his story is a good example of my philosophy that *all* life is precious, that *every* living being deserves an opportunity to live out its days in peace. And that's why I am so happy to have a thriving Peace Plantation operating in Walton, New York, and a healthy National Humane Education Society, working hard to protect animals all across our great nation.

## A Day in the Life of Peace Plantation

If you were to visit Peace Plantation, you'd drive into the countryside, taking New York State Route 206 to our facility. You'd see a huge barn amidst the lush, rolling hills, with several additions built on to accommodate the 600 cats and 50 dogs in residence at any given time. When you walked through the barn doors, you'd be amazed: Though so many animals live in this big structure, there's not a whiff of animal odor there, because the Peace Plantation staff lovingly keeps every kennel, every square foot of space scrupulously clean.

You'd see the cats in their large, airy enclosures, roaming at will, playing on freestanding treehouses or cuddling in wicker baskets or bunks. You'd see immediately that these animals get a lot of love, whether they are with us for only a few days before being adopted by a suitable owner, or whether they are with us for the rest of their lives.

*In no case is a healthy animal ever put to sleep at Peace Plantation!*

Nor do we ever want to turn away an animal in need—no matter where, no matter why, no matter what condition the animal may be in. Of course, this means we have had to board animals at well-run public kennels.

The Peace Plantation daily routine begins at feeding time, 8:00 a.m., when our staff swings into operation. Staff members monitor the animals while they eat. If any animals do not eat, they are scheduled for a check by the veterinary technician, just to make sure they are okay.

Once a week, *all* the animals with a problem are checked over by our visiting veterinarian. But every day, our veterinary technicians and vet tech assistants are on hand to take care of the animals' routine needs. Each new animal coming into Peace Plantation must be checked carefully, immunized, and neutered or spayed if she or he has not been already. That's a lot of care to be given! And all the healthy residents must be cared for, too: petted and talked to, brushed, played with. Some need their nails trimmed or their ears cleaned.

Meanwhile, the feeding dishes must be washed, the animals' areas cleaned, rugs and blankets laundered, and fresh water provided. And the Peace Plantation administrative staff must make sure we are well stocked with food and veterinary supplies, that our facility remains in good repair, and that we respond to the many, many calls for help we get every day. They work, too, to find good homes for our precious charges, and to encourage the local community to use our spay and neuter clinic. Services there are provided absolutely free of charge, as are all of our Society's services, though of course we do hope for donations.

People sometimes say we should charge for the services we provide, but I disagree. The National Humane Education Society is a true charity. When we start putting price tags on our services, people will stop providing their generous, heartfelt donations. I believe we get more support by not demanding payment. Our policy is best for the poor whose animals need help. And my belief has been borne out by the kindness of so many donors across America . . . people who have never even seen our Peace Plantation!

I've been tempted sometimes, though, to ask for payment for our services—only because our funds sometimes get so low, especially in winter, when the animals need us so much. We scramble to find space for them. Ultimately, we plan to build a new, larger facility at Peace Plantation on the 120-acre site we own.

But that's just part of the National Humane

Education Society's overall plan. And Peace Plantation is just one part of the work we do.

## *Meanwhile, Back in Leesburg . . .*

While my daughter, Virginia, and her husband, Earl Dungan, oversee the operation of Peace Plantation, with the assistance of our 22 indispensable and dedicated staff members, our headquarters staff in Leesburg keeps up its own hectic pace.

I still live near Leesburg myself, keeping a number of animals in a facility close by in West Virginia. But I spend most of my time—seven days a week, in fact—working for the Society.

That means I might be in our modest offices in Leesburg with our hard-working staff. What does my typical day include? Just about anything! I might be writing letters to editors of magazines like *Reader's Digest* to protest pro-vivisection articles on behalf of the Society's members. I might be driving to another state to pick up a family of cats whose owner can no longer care for them, since she is dying of cancer, or forced to enter a nursing home.

I might be out talking to people about issues. I might be writing an article for our *Quarterly Journal*, which goes to 130,000 people across America, our most important educational vehicle.

I might be talking to schoolchildren or civic groups about the importance of responsible pet ownership or other humane issues. I might be peacefully picketing a research laboratory with other Society members, asking them to stop putting animals through needless torture.

Or I might be sitting down with our managing consultant, Mr. William Kropp, to figure out how to make up the difference between our expenses—always growing, just as the number of animals in need continues to grow—and our income.

That financial crunch is always a worry, especially with so many animals in need of our help. But we of the National Humane Education Society have been blessed by the support of many kind men and women, especially in recent years. In fact, in January of 1988, I found myself in Mr. Kropp's office, stunned by an important realization.

"I can't believe it," I told him. "In the 39 years of the Society's existence, this is the first time."

Unintentionally, I left poor Mr. Kropp guessing for a few moments of silence.

"The first time for what?" he asked me.

"Why, here it is, the first of the year," I said slowly, "and all our bills are paid. That has never happened before!"

I must confess I shed a tear or two that day. All my life I have gone begging to get the money needed to keep our animals alive and well. I have not wanted to do it, but seeing no alternative, I have done it willingly. And of course in all the years I have worked for the Society, I have been a volunteer, foregoing any kind of salary or honoraria. I have done that willingly, too, though it meant my working another full-time job for many years.

Now, because the word has spread about our work, thousands of kind people across America have come to our aid. This has just happened in the last few years, and I am unbelievably grateful.

At last, at the ripe young age of 80, I could stop begging!

Still, our needs are many. Often, urgent calls to Peace Plantation ask us to take in one more homeless dog . . . one more family of kittens that will surely die if we don't take them in. We stretch the budget as thin as we can, and we manage to do what must be done. But I live with the fear that one day we may have to say "no"—that we may no longer be able to help.

When these worries overtake me, I think of my late husband and his never-ending optimism. I think of Ruby Brown and her tireless love for our animals. And I think to myself, "Not only will we never turn away a needy animal—but we're going to serve more and more animals! We're going to dream big!"

After all, God's lesser creatures need someone to speak for them. Every day, more beautiful animals need our help. We *must* look to the future on their behalf.

That is why I want to share my big dreams with you.

## The Future of the National Humane Education Society

As I write these words, Peace Plantation has many urgent needs. So when I say we no longer need to beg, I mean only that I am freed from the daily worry that our animals might not be fed. We are still operating on a shoestring, as efficiently as possible. The only volunteers we have are several caring ladies who often visit just to pet the animals.

Right now, we're in need of a new Peace Plantation vehicle for rescuing and transporting animals. We have two road-worthy vehicles at the Sanctuary. One is a van with 78,000 miles on it and the other is a covered truck with 140,000 miles, both of which often make the 300-mile round trip to New York City several times a week, for rescues. We have a truck with 300,000 miles on it that's still running, and a Jeep we've had since 1979. We use these as farm vehicles only—they're not safe to take on the road.

Also, and perhaps most urgently, we need more housing for our animals. I'd love not to have to board out any animals, even temporarily, because it costs so much more to do so. And, as the demand for our services grows, I want to be ready to accommodate *every* animal who needs us. We can only hope to do this if we can build new buildings at our Walton facility, *and*—my fondest dream—establish another Peace Plantation near our headquarters in Leesburg, Virginia.

Optimistic people say "*when* it happens," not "*if* it happens." So I'll phrase my dream this way: *When* we build our second Peace Plantation near Leesburg, I hope we can also fulfill a very old dream of mine by building a national humane education center. Here, children of all ages (up to 100 years and more!) could come and get to know animals, see exhibits about humane treatment of animals, and learn how to fulfill their responsibilities to God's precious creatures, whether they be hummingbirds or humpback whales.

No such center exists in the United States today,

and I have longed to build it for over 30 years. Now it is my hope that we will be able to do so—with help from kind people who love animals.

## Speaking for Those Who Cannot Speak for Themselves

Of course, there's another major part of our Society's work: animal advocacy. In this book, you have read about the many outrages perpetrated on animals today, from neglect and abandonment to the staged cruelty of bullfights, from the torture condoned by supposedly great scientists to the agony of fur-bearing creatures caught in vicious traps, from the death of 10 million unwanted puppies and kittens each year to the shrinking environment which will wipe out *all* animal life someday, including humans, unless we do something now.

The work we do is *vital*, and we are in a better position to do it now than ever before, because our membership has swollen to over 130,000 men and women across the United States. Now, we can rally our forces and make a difference when pro-animal legislation is before Congress. Now, we can stand up and speak for the animals who cannot speak for themselves. And with our combined voices, we can make a real difference.

For me, this is a continuation of the work Briggsie did in the 1920s, '30s, and '40s, the work he was doing on the day he died. It is the crusade whose success or failure will determine the future of billions of animals—even the future of our planet. For if we, the human race, do not care about animal life, then we do not care about life itself. And we will prove it ultimately by destroying our beautiful planet.

Animal advocacy and our rescue and shelter work is the mission of my life, the work I hope to be engaged in until I die, the work I hope will continue long beyond my lifetime, shepherded by the caring, dedicated people who now help me run the National Humane Education Society. My daughter, Virginia Dungan, has voiced her hope of carrying on the work of her parents. She has served as the Vice President of the National Humane Education Society since 1983.

I'm hopeful that Peace Plantation is the kind of place today that Briggsie envisioned when he started his Be Kind to Animals Rest Farm in 1920. And I hope, too, that he is proud to see the National Humane Education Society's strong membership rallying in support of the causes he championed. I dare to hope that he is looking down from his Heavenly home and giving us his blessing.

Because I love animals so much, dear reader, I'm bold enough to hope that you, too, will give us your blessing . . . that you will support our Society in all its work by making a donation of any size today. You can rest assured that it will be put to good use immediately. If you can possibly arrange to visit our office in Leesburg, Virginia or our sanctuary at Walton, New York, please do so.

If you'd like to help us help the animals, please send your check, made payable to the National Humane Education Society, to me at the following address:

Anna C. Briggs, President
National Humane Education Society
15-B Catoctin Circle, SE, Room 207
Leesburg, VA 22075
703-777-8319

It would be an honor and a privilege to have the opportunity to thank you . . . on behalf of the animals!

# CHAPTER 11

# Our Call to Conscience: Alice Morgan Wright's Humane Principles

*In 1963, Miss Alice Morgan Wright, co-founder of the National Humane Education Society, wrote the following article, in which she describes her convictions about the humane treatment of animals. These principles have become the cornerstone of the National Humane Education Society. May they inspire you as they have inspired me over these many years.*

—Anna C. Briggs

For many years I have pondered the problem of how I might most effectively continue to help animals and to support humane principles after I am gone from this earth. The fruit of my study and thought is a will bequeathing all that I have to a selected list of humane societies throughout the world and to the Alice Morgan Wright-Edith J. Goode Foundation for

Animal Welfare, which will use permanent funds of the Foundation to assist needy humane societies that follow genuine humane principles. For the friends and the humane organizations that are to receive bequests and future grants under my will, and for all friends and defenders of animals, I have tried to assemble a few thoughts and recommendations gleaned from experiences in my long life.

I have become convinced that the worst of all crimes committed are acts of cruelty, and of all the cruelties the most excruciating is that perpetrated by experimenters upon living animals. The recorded tortures of human beings are seldom of such long duration as those inflicted upon some laboratory animals. Some suffer from repeated experiments for months, even for years.

At this very time means are being sought to limit the increase of human population in most parts of the world. Over-population has been called a greater menace to mankind than the atom bomb itself. Yet the justification of vivisection and the torture of animals is alleged by the researchers to be the possibility of finding ways to save human life and to prolong the lives of the very old and helpless.

Cruelty is inflicted also in the name of sport. Each country has its favorite cruel spectacles. Rodeo is billed as that "good, clean, American sport." Cock-fighting is popular. Dog-fighting to the death is enjoyed by some. Rabbit killings by stoning and beating with clubs, in which men, women and children participate, are a traditional festival of a chapter of a well-known organization in our country. We have the coon-on-a-log, the coyote in a pen, to be attacked and killed by dogs for the enjoyment of the spectators.

Since these events are the delight of our public, it is almost impossible to obtain an injunction or a criminal judgment from our courts, although anti-cruelty laws on the books in the states where these events occur forbid the beating of an animal and other abuses.

All of these facts indicate to me that the only hope for the relief of animals is through the long, hard process of educating the human race, from childhood onward, by the teaching of compassion. Let us remember the great gifts of companionship and of beauty which are ours through association with living creatures of Earth and ask ourselves how such sentient flesh could have been thought suitable for sacrifice by torture in experiments endlessly repeated in laboratory after laboratory.

By what right does one sentient being torture another? Does the God of the Christians sanction it? Is it justified even by the hope of prolonging human life in an era when over-population threatens the health and the subsistence of mankind?

In Genesis I, 26 and 28, it is reported that God gave Man "dominion" over the animals. Some modern scholars have asserted that the English word nearer to the original meaning would be *responsibility*. If in those two verses the Church had read that God gave Man *responsibility* for the animals, how different would have been the attitude of the Church and the faithful toward animals, and how much easier would be our task of teaching compassion and the prevention of cruelty to animals.

There is one possibility of educating the next generation of the human race in compassion, in our era of speed, through the United Nations' UNESCO and its program of world education. Let us appeal to UNESCO again, and repeatedly, to include humane education in that program. The concepts of compassion common to the utterances of the prophets, the poets, the philosophers of the races of men should be translated into all tongues for all children to understand.

To bring this international teaching of compassion into our own schoolrooms is our duty; to promote insistently in our institutions of learning the education of the heart, and the courage to withstand any popular trend which, in the misused name of Science, might lead to disregard for the fundamental ethics of righteousness and compassion.

In order that this teaching of the school shall obtain also in the home it is important to urge parents and other guardians of children to take the greatest care in avoiding cruelty and hardship to the animals with which the children are associated.

For putting into practice my thoughts and recommendations I would set down the following reminders—the ways and means:

1. To oppose cruelty in all its forms.

2. To strive for an end to bullfighting, rodeo, and all cruel sports wherever performed and wherever represented as art or as entertainment.

3. To strive to abolish cruel trapping. (In my estimation there could be no such thing as a "humane trap." The words are a contradiction in terms. Only a box-trap should be tolerated.)

4. To discourage hunting, especially as a sport.

5. To oppose all poisoning of wildlife.

6. To protect and conserve wildlife for its own sake and not as a resource for Man's exploitation.

7. To aid or initiate programs for slaughter reform.

8. To teach humane handling and care of work animals and food animals.

9. To cooperate in efforts to find more humane methods of catching and killing the fauna of the sea, especially whales and seals.

10. To advance programs for the humane sterilization of cats and dogs in order to reduce their overpopulation.

11. To provide for the rescue, housing and feeding of lost, stray or abandoned animals, until suitable homes are found.

12. To urge that when it is necessary to put any tame animal to death, unless some better method of euthanasia is available, it be so arranged that the animal be held in the arms of some human friend while it is being given a painless preliminary anaesthetic, to be stroked and comforted with reassuring words until it loses consciousness, after which the lethal agent should be quickly administered.

13. To recognize in animals their capacity for friendship and their need of friends. To befriend all Earth's creatures, of the land, the sea and the air; to defend them against ravages by mankind, and to inspire in human beings compassion for all.

—Alice Morgan Wright
Albany, New York
January 1963